Get Your LACE On

LEISURE ARTS, INC. • Maumelle, Arkansas

Meet the DESIGNER

By Melissa Leapman

Makers all over the world know the joy of creating beautiful and useful items using their own hands. With fashion houses in my hometown of New York City currently featuring lots of trendy lace garments, particularly in super hot yarns, it's time to get your lace on!

Although lace patterns might appear especially complicated, they're actually easy and fun to knit. The patterns are created by working a balance of YO increases and simple decreases. (Finally, a reason to make intentional holes in your knitting!)

In this book, I'll walk you through all the basics from beginning to end, from casting on to binding off. Clear photos will show you exactly how to do everything, and the 18 projects will allow you to practice and showcase your new skills.

Every pattern is written in both text and chart form. Some knitters prefer the visual presentation of charts while others like the explicit words. In this book, the choice is yours!

My recent book, *Knitting Modular Shawls* (Storey Publishing, 2018) explores the beauty of lace shawls and wraps for beginners and avid knitters. But *Get Your Lace On!* lets you discover other types of lace projects, from sweaters to scarves to cowls and more.

There's magic in every ball of yarn. Let's add a few YOs to a little bit of creativity and watch things get really fun Find me on Instagram as Melissa.Leapman and on Ravelry as MelissaLeapman. I look forward to knitting with you!

CONTENTS

Essential Techniques For Lace Knitting

Lace is one of those cool knitting techniques that looks much more complicated than it is. These openwork patterns and motifs are created simply by adding holes to a solid fabric!

MATERIALS

Lace knitting doesn't require any special materials, however following are some things to make learning and knitting these special fabrics super easy and fun.

Yarn

Nearly any yarn can be used for lace knitting. Traditionally, fine yarns were used, but using thicker yarns: even super chunky weight: yields a more modern-looking fabric with lots of pop. The *Hat* on page 14, for example, uses bulky weight yarn and size 10½ (6.5 mm) needles. You can make it in a day or two!

Smooth yarns work best, since they allow the beautiful stitchwork to shine. I stay away from most novelty yarns such as eyelash, thick-and-thin yarn, and tweeds for this reason.

Needles

Obviously, any type of knitting needle works for lace, but since you'll be doing lots of decreases, the pointier the tip, the better. That makes it easier to get the tip into two or three stitches at once. Believe it or not, every manufacturer's needle tips have a unique shape. Choose the ones that work best for you.

Another thing to consider is the material used to make your knitting needles. For beginners, I always recommend wood or bamboo tools. These needles are slightly sticky and make it easier to avoid dropping stitches, the bane of every knitter's existence.

Not that knitting is a race, but for speed knitting, metal needles are useful. Their slippery surface allows stitches to glide quickly and easily.

Plastic or resin needles work universally because they're neither too "grabby" nor too slick. I always have a set of plastic interchangeable needles in my project bag.

The type of project you're knitting will determine whether your needles should be straight or circular. When knitting in the round, you'll use circular needles, of course. But for flat projects that call for a large number of stitches, such as the *Two-Color Shawl* on page 34, a long circular needle is best. In this case, don't join at the end of the rows; instead, just work back and forth in rows. The flexible needle accommodates the large number of stitches.

GAUGE

Gauge refers to the number of stitches and rows per inch in your knitted fabric, and it depends on the size of each individual stitch. It is essential to understand how gauge works in order to control the finished size of your knitted projects.

Many things affect the size of your stitches, from the size of your yarn to the size of your needles, to the material your needles are made of. Even your mood can affect your gauge: knitting nervously during a horror movie will likely result in a tighter gauge than knitting while relaxing in front of a fireplace on vacation.

Commercial patterns, including those in this book, are written for a particular gauge. If you want your finished project to be the same size as the one listed in the Finished Measurements section of the pattern (and fit like the project photographed), be sure to match the gauge called for exactly. Even the difference of one-half of a stitch per inch could make your piece several inches larger or smaller than you expect. (Ask me how I know!) You might have to knit several gauge swatches using different needle sizes to obtain the perfect gauge. Don't skip this crucial step! Remember: any knitting time is fun! Even swatch knitting!

Typically, patterns will indicate the desired gauge over four inches rather than over one inch. Measuring over a larger width yields a more accurate determination of the gauge of the fabric since individual stitches tend to vary slightly in size, even for the most experienced knitters.

If you find it difficult to measure your gauge in a fabric worked in a pattern stitch such as lace, cast on a few repeats of the pattern and work for about six inches and then bind off. It'll be easy to measure the width and height of one stitch repeat, and you can use that information to determine how many stitches you have per inch.

If you plan to block your finished pieces ***(page 9)***, be sure to block your gauge swatches as well. As it refines the fabric and makes your stitches look uniform, it also changes the size and shape of stitches, affecting the gauge.

To accurately measure your gauge, knit a gauge swatch in the stitch pattern used for the project, bind off all stitches, and then use rust-proof pins (trust me!) to secure the fabric to a flat surface (blocking mats or a folded-up bath towel will work). Be sure that your piece of knitted fabric is at least 5" (12.5 cm) square, since you will want to avoid the edge stitches on all sides of the fabric when measuring. These edge stitches: called selvedge stitches: tend to be wonky and uneven in size and are not representative of most of your fabric. Besides, they will be hidden within the seams (if any) of your project and will not affect its finished measurements.

Count the number of stitches over 4" (10 cm), staying away from all edges of the fabric, and avoid pressing down too hard on the fabric.

If you have fewer stitches per inch than what is called for in the pattern, knit another swatch with smaller knitting needles; if you have more stitches, then try again with larger ones. When knitting, it doesn't matter what size knitting needles you use, only that your gauge matches the one called for in the pattern.

BEGINNING AND ENDING LACE

Since lace projects are often blocked when completed, it is important to have relatively loose cast on and bind off edges. Here are some of my favorite methods.

Simple Cast On

To achieve a stretchy cast on I usually just use larger needles (up one or two sizes) with my regular cast on technique: long tail or knit on. The larger needles allow for extra give when blocking ***(see page 9)***.

Beginning Ring

I use this method when casting on just a few stitches in the round, such as for the *Baby Blanket* on page 78. It's great because it makes it so easy to neatly tighten the center hole.

Here's how: Make a loop in the yarn, keeping the working yarn from the ball on top and a 6" (15 cm) tail underneath ***(Photo A)***. ★ Insert a crochet hook in the center of the loop, then use it to reach up and grab the working yarn coming out of the ball ***(Photo B)***. Draw the working yarn through the middle of the loop ***(Photo C)***, then wrap the yarn around the hook once more and draw it through the loop on the hook ***(Photo D)***. Repeat from the ★ as many times as necessary to cast on the specified number of stitches ***(Photo E)***. Distribute these stitches onto double-pointed needles or a circular needle to begin knitting. Finally, tug on the yarn tail to tighten the loop.

Super Stretchy Bind Off

This technique leaves an elastic edge that's perfect for projects that will be blocked such as the *Mandala Shawl* on page 70.

Here's how: K2, ★ return the 2 sts back to the left needle, K2 tog tbl ***(Photo F)***, K1; repeat from ★ across until all sts have been bound off.

Photo A

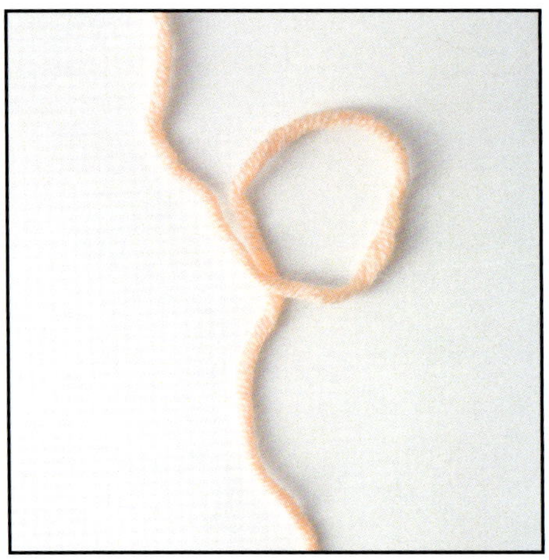

Photo B

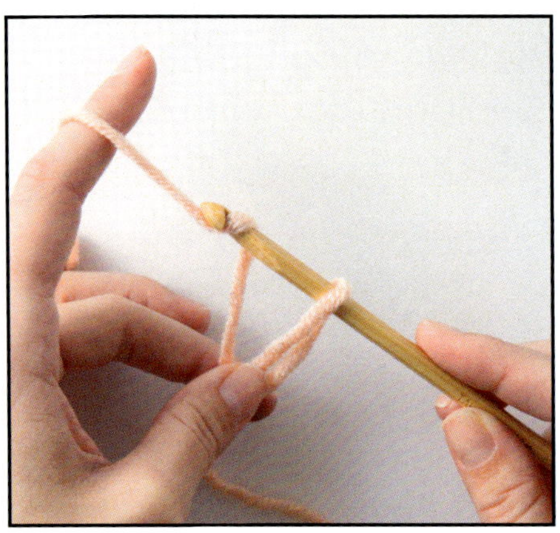

Photo C

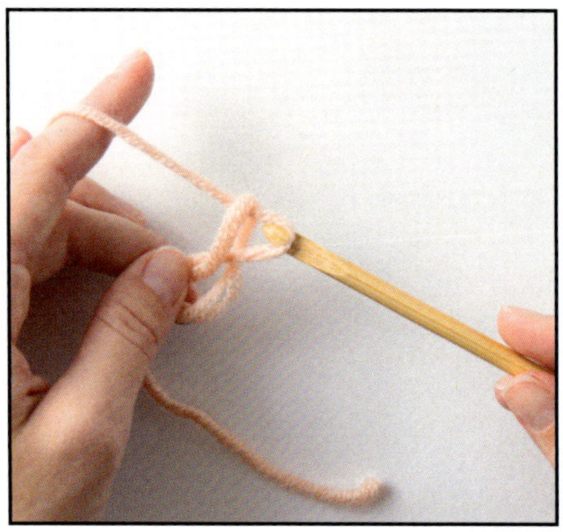

Photo D

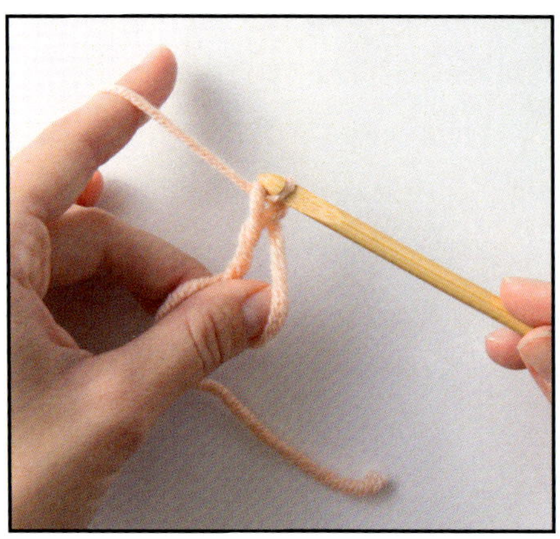

Photo E

Photo F

LACE CONSTRUCTION

Lace designs use YO stitches to intentionally add delicate holes to the fabric. When knitting these openwork patterns, YO increases are balanced with decreases in order to keep the stitch count constant. As intricate as some lace patterns might appear, they're relatively easy to knit! (Sssshhhhhh. Let's keep that secret just between us!)

The increases are predominately YO stitches; the decreases are usually knit two together ***(abbreviated K2 tog)*** and slip slip knit ***(abbreviated SSK)***. These decreases are perfect mirror images of each other and are the secret to the lovely patternwork.

Here are the increases and decreases you will encounter in lace knitting.

Increases

To make a yarn over between two knit stitches: The working yarn is in the **back**. Bring it between the two needle tips to the **front** ***(Photo G)***. As you knit the next stitch, the yarn will go over the right-hand needle, creating the yarn over.

To make a yarn over between a knit and a purl stitch: The working yarn is in the **back**. Bring it between the two needle tips to the **front**, and then wrap it all the way around the right-hand needle to the **front** again ***(Photo H)***.

To make a yarn over between a purl and a knit stitch: The working yarn is in the front. As you knit the next stitch, the yarn will go over the right-hand needle, creating the yarn over ***(Photo I)***.

To make a yarn over between two purl stitches: The working yarn is in the **front**. Wrap it all the way around the right-hand needle to the **front** creating the yarn over ***(Photo J)***.

Decreases

To knit two together *(abbreviated K2 tog)*: With the working yarn in the **back**, insert the tip of the right-hand needle into two stitches **at once** as if to **knit** ***(Photo K)***. Wrap the yarn around to complete the stitch as a knit stitch. *This decrease slants to the right.*

Photo G

Photo H

Photo I

Photo J

Photo K

To slip, slip, knit *(abbreviated SSK)*: With the working yarn in the **back**, insert the right-hand needle from the left to the right (knitwise), into the first and second stitches on the left needle, *one at a time*, and slip them onto the right needle ***(Photo L)***. Then, insert the tip of the left-hand needle into the **front** of both slipped stitches ***(Photo M)*** and knit them together from this position, through their back loops. *This decrease slants to the left.*

To knit three stitches together *(abbreviated K3 tog)*: With the working yarn in the **back**, insert the tip of the right-hand needle into three stitches **at once** as if to **knit**. Complete the same as a K2 tog. *This double decrease slants to the right.*

To slip, slip, slip, knit *(abbreviated SSSK)*: With the working yarn in the **back**, insert the right-hand needle from the left to the right (knitwise), into the first, second and third stitches on the left needle, *one at a time*, and slip them onto the right needle. Complete same as a SSK. *This double decrease slants to the left.*

To make a slip two together, knit one, pass two slipped stitches over *(abbreviated S2KP2)*: With the working yarn in the **back**, insert the right-hand needle into the next 2 stitches **at once** as if to do a K2 tog, and slip them onto the right-hand needle ***(Photo N)***. Knit the next stitch the regular way, then pass the 2 slipped stitches over the stitch you just knitted ***(Photo O)***. *This double decrease is vertical and has no slant **(Photo P)**.*

Photo L

Photo M

Photo N

Photo O

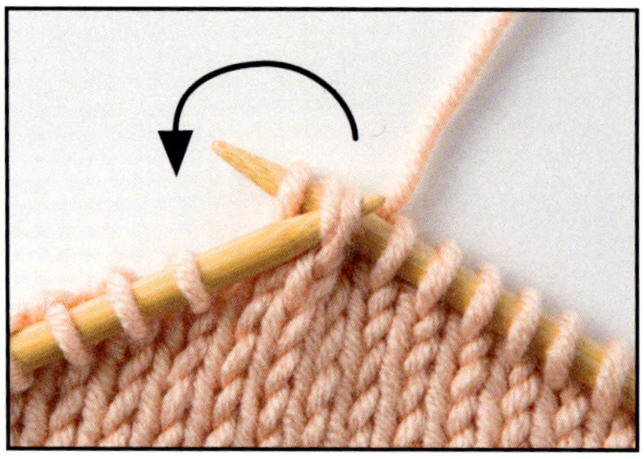

Photo P

Slanted Decreases

If you find it difficult to remember which decrease leans to the left and which one leans to the right you're not alone! Here's an easy way to keep them straight:

Write out the abbreviated names of the decreases "K2 tog" and "SSK". Then, draw a diagonal line through the right slant of the "2" and through the left slant of the "s" as shown.

The K2 tog leans to the right and the SSK leans to the left. Easy!

k2tog
(slants to the right)

ssk
(slants to the left)

FINISHING TECHNIQUES

After all the knitting is completed, good finishing techniques will ensure that your project will look perfect.

Blocking

Blocking is a finishing process that helps "set" any knitted project to your desired size. It evens out the stitches, magically making the overall fabric look uniformly knit. In lace projects, blocking opens up the fabric, making it airy and beautiful, emphasizing the patternwork. Knitters have several methods of blocking, but wet-blocking is the one I like best.

To do: Launder the knitted piece, being sure to follow the manufacturer's instructions on the yarn label. Lay the piece flat on a padded surface out of direct sunlight, patting it gently to your desired measurements. Using rust-proof pins, pin the damp fabric down and allow it to dry completely.

Dealing With Yarn Ends

Yarn tails are a necessary evil in knitting. Here's how to take care of them so they are invisible and secure.

Use a pointed-end yarn needle to make short running stitches on the **wrong** side of your fabric in a diagonal line for about 1" (2.5 cm) or so, piercing the yarn strands that comprise the stitches of your fabric. Then, work back again to where you began, working alongside your previous running stitches. Finally, to secure the tail, work a stitch or two and actually pierce the stitches you just created. Be sure to work each tail individually, in opposite diagonal directions, and you will secure your yarn ends while keeping the public side of your fabric beautiful.

Pro Tips

for Knitting from Charts

- Use a sticky note to help keep track of where you are on the chart. Place it above the row you are working and move it up after you complete each row.
- Place markers on the knitting needle after each stitch repeat; it'll make it easy to count your stitches.
- Use a highlighter to color in each wrong side row. This will be a visual clue that the symbols on these rows must be mentally reversed when knitting.

LACE CHARTS 101

While I've included all patterns in this book in both text and chart form, I encourage you to try to wean yourself off the written-out versions. Once you get accustomed to using them, knitting charts can make your stitching easier, faster, and more fun.

How They Work

Knitting charts are a visual representation of the public side of knitted fabric.

Each square of the grid corresponds to one stitch and each row of squares corresponds to one row (or round) of stitches.

Charts are read in the same way that the fabric is knit: from the lower edge up, with the first row at the bottom of the chart and the last row at the top.

Right side rows are read from **right** to **left**, in the same order that stitches present themselves to you on the left-hand knitting needle.

At the end of this first row, you flip your knitting before starting the next row, and the **wrong** side of the fabric faces you. Physically, the first stitch of this **wrong** side row is the same stitch as the last stitch of the right-side row you just completed. Thus, **wrong side** rows on charts are read in the opposite direction, from **left** to **right**.

Note: When working in the round rather than back and forth in rows, such as for the *Hat* on page 14 and the *Striped Cowl* on page 12, the right side of the fabric is always facing you, so **all** rows of the chart are read from **right** to **left**.

Charts make it easy to see how many stitches are involved in a pattern. In some charts, a bold box sets off the stitch repeat, and if extra stitches are required on each side to center the pattern on the fabric, they are shown to the left and right of the repeat.

In the *Little Top* on page 42, for example, the Eyelet Rib pattern has a multiple of four stitches plus one stitch; it is a four-stitch repeat with one "balancing" stitch on the right-hand side. This stitch sits outside the stitch repeat and so is worked once per row. It is the first stitch of every right side row, and since wrong side rows are read from left-to-right, it is the last stitch of these rows.

Symbols

Each symbol on a chart indicates the way a stitch will be worked, and the arrangement of the symbols on the chart determines the stitch pattern.

Usually, the symbols visually resemble the way the resulting stitches will appear on the public side of the knitted fabric. The symbol for a knit stitch, for example, is a blank box, mimicking the flat appearance of the knit stitch itself; the dot symbol for a purl stitch depicts the bumpy appearance of a purled stitch. *Refer to the symbol key near each chart for easy translation.*

All symbols are shown in charts as they appear on the public side of the fabric. This means that the same symbol means different things on **right** and **wrong** side rows. The blank box, for instance, represents a knit stitch on a **right** side row, but if you're on a **wrong** side row and want the stitch to appear as a knit stitch on the reverse side of the fabric, you must purl it.

Often, wrong side rows are pretty simple: you just knit the knit stitches and purl the purl stitches and YO stitches as they present themselves to you on the knitting needle. Scan the entire chart before you begin knitting to confirm that this is the case. If so, you can zip along those "rest rows" reading your knitting rather than the chart!

Projects

Here are 18 lace projects to practice and showcase your new skills ***(pages 12-89)***. Makers gotta make!

Striped Cowl

●●○○ **EASY**

Finished Measurement:
9½" high x 22" circumference
(24 cm x 56 cm)

SHOPPING LIST

Yarn (Medium Weight)

[3½ ounces, 198 yards
(100 grams, 181 meters) per skein]:

- ☐ Cream - 1 skein
- ☐ Terra Cotta - 1 skein
- ☐ Gray - 1 skein

Knitting Needles

16" (40.5 cm) Circular,

- ☐ Size 8 (5 mm)
  or size needed for gauge

Additional Supplies

- ☐ Stitch marker
- ☐ Yarn needle

GAUGE INFORMATION

In pattern,
22 sts and 24 rows/rnds = 4" (10 cm)

TECHNIQUES USED

- YO *(Photo G, page 7)*
- K2 tog *(Photo K, page 7)*
- SSK *(Photos L & M, page 8)*

COLOR SEQUENCE

★ 6 rounds of Cream, 6 rounds of Terra Cotta, 6 rounds of Gray; repeat from ★ for stripe sequence.

COWL

With Cream, cast on 121 sts; place marker to indicate beginning of rnd *(see Markers and Circular Knitting, pages 91 & 92)*.

Rnd 1 (Right side)**:** ★ K2 tog twice, YO, (K1, YO) 3 times, SSK twice; repeat from ★ around.

Rnd 2: Purl around.

Rnd 3: ★ K2 tog twice, YO, (K1, YO) 3 times, SSK twice; repeat from ★ around.

Rnds 4-6: Knit around.

Working in Color Sequence, repeat Rnds 1-6 for pattern until Cowl measures approximately 9½" (24 cm) from cast on edge, ending by working 6 rnds of any color.

Bind off all sts **loosely** in pattern.

CHART

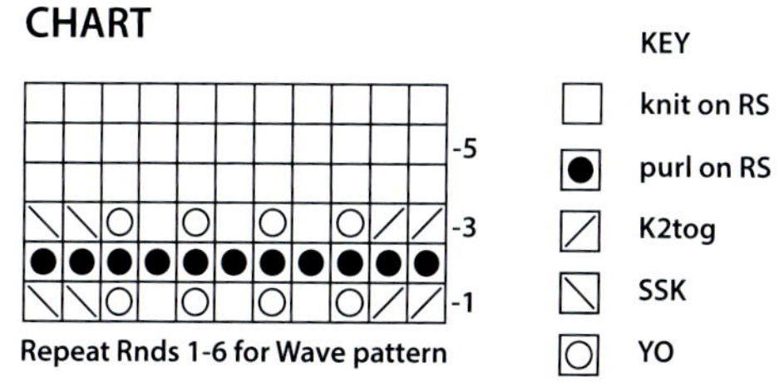

Repeat Rnds 1-6 for Wave pattern

Follow chart from right to left on all rnds.

Slouchy Hat

●●○○ **EASY**

Finished Size: 18" (45.5 cm) circumference

SHOPPING LIST

Yarn (Bulky Weight) BULKY 5

[7 ounces, 247 yards (200 grams, 226 meters) per skein]:

☐ 1 skein

Knitting Needles

16" (40.5 cm) Circular,

☐ Size 9 (5.5 mm) **and**

☐ Size 10½ (6.5 mm)

or sizes needed for gauge

Double-pointed needles,

☐ Size 10½ (6.5 mm) (for Crown Shaping)

Additional Supplies

☐ Stitch marker

☐ Yarn needle

☐ Pom-pom (optional)

GAUGE INFORMATION

With larger size needles, in pattern, 13 sts and 20 rows = 4" (10 cm)

TECHNIQUES USED

- YO ***(Photo G, page 7)***
- K2 tog ***(Photo K, page 7)***
- SSK ***(Photos L & M, page 8)***

HAT

Ribbing

With smaller size circular needle, cast on 72 sts; place a marker to indicate the beginning of the round ***(see Markers and Circular Knitting, pages 91 & 92).***

Work in (K2, P2) ribbing around for 1½" (4 cm).

Body

Change to larger size circular needle.

Rnd 1 (Right side)**:** ★ K4, K2 tog, YO, K3, YO, SSK, K1; repeat from ★ around.

Rnd 2 AND ALL EVEN NUMBERED RNDS TO CROWN SHAPING: Knit around.

Rnd 3: ★ K3, K2 tog, YO, K1, YO, SSK, K4; repeat from ★ around.

Rnd 5: ★ K2, K2 tog, YO, K3, YO, SSK, K3; repeat from ★ around.

Rnd 7: ★ K5, K2 tog, YO, K1, YO, SSK, K2; repeat from ★ around.

Repeat Rnds 1-8 for pattern until Hat measures approximately 9½" (24 cm) from cast on edge, ending by working Rnd 8.

CHART

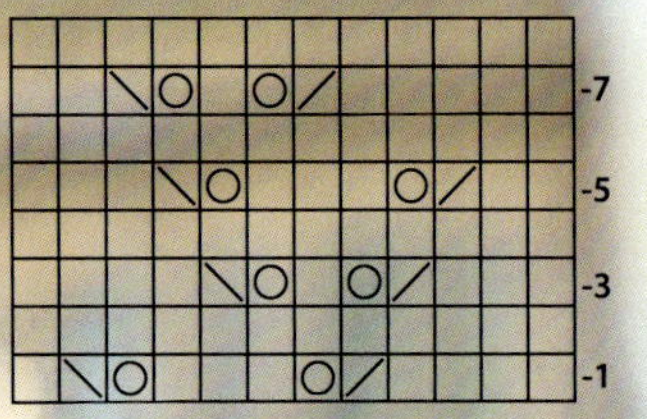

KEY

☐ knit on RS

◿ K2 tog

◺ SSK

◯ YO

Repeat Rnds 1-8 for pattern

Follow chart from right to left on all rnds.

CROWN SHAPING

Rnd 1: ★ SSK, K4, K2 tog, K4; repeat from ★ around: 60 sts.

Rnd 2: ★ SSK, K2, K2 tog, K4; repeat from ★ around: 48 sts.

Rnd 3: ★ SSK, K2 tog, K4; repeat from ★ around: 36 sts.

Rnd 4: ★ SSK, K1; repeat from ★ around: 24 sts.

Rnds 5 and 6: SSK around: 6 sts.

Cut yarn leaving a long end for sewing. Thread yarn needle with end and weave through remaining sts, gathering **tightly** to close.

Optional: Sew pom-pom to top of hat.

Cap Sleeve Top

●●○○ **EASY**

SHOPPING LIST

Yarn (Medium Weight) MEDIUM 4

[3½ ounces, 198 yards (100 grams, 181 meters) per skein]:

☐ {4-5-6}{7-8-9} skeins

Knitting Needles

Straight,

☐ Size 8 (5 mm)

or size needed for gauge

Additional Supplies

☐ Cable needle

☐ Stitch markers - 2

☐ Yarn needle

SIZE INFORMATION

Finished Bust Measurement:
{36-39¼-42½}{44¾-48¾-52}"/
{91.5-99.5-108}{114-124-132} cm

Finished Length:
{24½-24½-25}{25½-26-26½}"/
{62-62-63.5}{65-66-67.5} cm

Size Note: For ease in following the pattern, we have printed the instructions for each size in a different color:

- Size Small in Blue
- Size Medium in Pink
- Size Large in Green
- Size 1X in Red
- Size 2X in Purple
- Size 3X in Orange

Instructions in Black apply to all sizes.

GAUGE INFORMATION

In Stockinette Stitch,
20 sts and 24 rows = 4" (10 cm)

STITCH GUIDE

CABLE 8 BACK *(abbreviated C8B)* (uses 8 sts)

Slip next 4 sts onto cable needle and hold in **back** of work, K4 from left needle, K4 from cable needle.

CABLE 8 FRONT *(abbreviated C8F)* (uses 8 sts)

Slip next 4 sts onto cable needle and hold in **front** of work, K4 from left needle, K4 from cable needle.

TECHNIQUES USED

- YO ***(see Increases, page 7)***
- K2 tog ***(Photo K, page 7)***
- SSK ***(Photos L & M, page 8)***
- SSSK ***(see Decreases, page 8)***
- P2 tog ***(Fig. 10, page 94)***
- K3 tog ***(Fig. 11, page 94)***
- SSP ***(Fig. 12, page 94)***

BACK

Ribbing

Cast on {92-100-108}{114-124-132} sts.

Work in K1, P1 ribbing for 1" (2.5 cm).

Body

Row 1 (Right side)**:** Knit {34-38-42}{45-50-54} sts, place marker, P2, K5, K3 tog, YO, K1, YO, P2, YO, K1, YO, SSSK, K5, P2, place marker, knit {34-38-42}{45-50-54} sts.

Row 2 AND ALL WRONG SIDE ROWS: Purl to marker, slip marker, K2, (P9, K2) twice, slip marker, purl across.

Row 3: Knit to marker, slip marker, P2, K4, K3 tog, (YO, K1) twice, P2, (K1, YO) twice, SSSK, K4, P2, slip marker, knit across.

Row 5: Knit to marker, slip marker, P2, K3, K3 tog, YO, K1, YO, K2, P2, K2, YO, K1, YO, SSSK, K3, P2, slip marker, knit across.

Row 7: Knit to marker, slip marker, P2, K2, K3 tog, YO, K1, YO, K3, P2, K3, YO, K1, YO, SSSK, K2, P2, slip marker, knit across.

Row 9: Knit to marker, slip marker, P2, K1, K3 tog, YO, K1, YO, K4, P2, K4, YO, K1, YO, SSSK, K1, P2, slip marker, knit across.

Row 11: Knit to marker, slip marker, P2, K3 tog, YO, K1, YO, K5, P2, K5, YO, K1, YO, SSSK, P2, slip marker, knit across.

Row 13: Knit to marker, slip marker, P2, C8B, K1, P2, K1, C8F, P2, slip marker, knit across.

Row 15 Knit to marker, slip marker, P2, K5, K3 tog, YO, K1, YO, P2, YO, K1, YO, SSSK, K5, P2, slip marker, knit across.

Repeat Rows 2-15 for pattern until Back measures approximately 16½" (42 cm) from cast on edge, ending by working a **wrong** side row.

ARMHOLE SHAPING

Note: Maintain established pattern throughout.

Row 1 (Decrease row)**:** K1, SSK, work across to last 3 sts, K2 tog, K1: {90-98-106}{112-122-130} sts.

Sizes Small, Large, and 1X ONLY

Row 2: Purl to marker, slip marker, K2, (P9, K2) twice, slip marker, purl across.

Row 3: Repeat Row 1: {88-104}{110} sts.

CHART

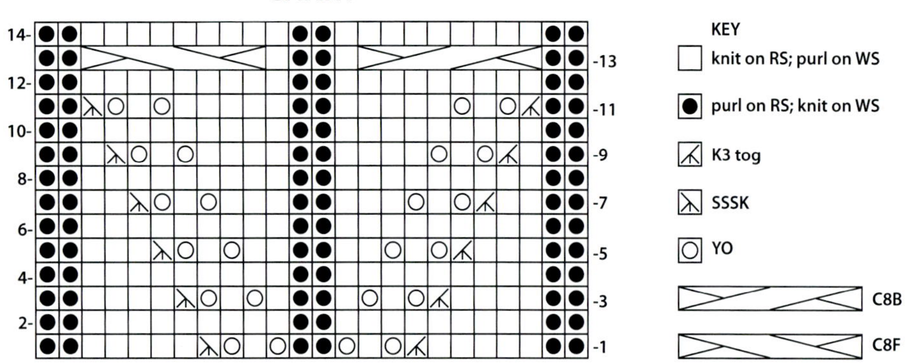

Repeat Rows 1-14 for pattern
Follow chart from right to left on RS rows;
follow chart from left to right on WS rows.

Size Small ONLY

Rows 4-9: Repeat Rows 2 and 3, 3 times: 82 sts.

All Sizes

Next Row (Wrong side)**:** P1, P2 tog, work across to last 3 sts, SSP, P1: {80-96-102}{108-120-128} sts.

Next Row: Repeat Row 1: {78-94-100}{106-118-126} sts.

Continue to decrease one st at each edge every row until {46-46-46}{50-50-56} sts remain.

Size 3X ONLY

Next Row: K1, SSSK, work across to last 4 sts, K3 tog, K1: 52 sts.

All Sizes

Bind off all sts in pattern.

FRONT

Work same as Back.

SLEEVE (Make 2)

Ribbing

Cast on {64-64-68}{70-74-74} sts.

Work in K1, P1 ribbing for 1" (2.5 cm).

Body

Size 3X ONLY

Row 1 (Right side)**:** K 25, place marker, P2, K5, K3 tog, YO, K1, YO, P2, YO, K1, YO, SSSK, K5, P2, place marker, K 25.

Sizes Small, Medium, Large, 1X, and 2X ONLY

Row 1 (Right side)**:** K1, SSK, knit {17-17-19}{20-22} sts, place marker, P2, K5, K3 tog, YO, K1, YO, P2, YO, K1, YO, SSSK, K5, P2, place marker, knit {17-17-19}{20-22} sts, K2 tog, K1: {62-62-66}{68-72} sts.

All Sizes

Row 2: Purl to marker, slip marker, K2, (P9, K2) twice, slip marker, purl across.

Row 3: K1, SSK, knit to marker, slip marker, P2, K4, K3 tog, (YO, K1) twice, P2, (K1, YO) twice, SSSK, K4, P2, slip marker, knit across to last 3 sts, K2 tog, K1: {60-60-64}{66-70-72} sts.

Row 5: K1, SSK, knit to marker, slip marker, P2, K3, K3 tog, YO, K1, YO, K2, P2, K2, YO, K1, YO, SSSK, K3, P2, slip marker, knit across to last 3 sts, K2 tog, K1: {58-58-62}{64-68-70} sts.

Row 7: K1, SSK, knit to marker, slip marker, P2, K2, K3 tog, YO, K1, YO, K3, P2, K3, YO, K1, YO, SSSK, K2, P2, slip marker, knit across to last 3 sts, K2 tog, K1: {56-56-60}{62-66-68} sts.

Row 9: K1, SSK, knit to marker, slip marker, P2, K1, K3 tog, YO, K1, YO, K4, P2, K4, YO, K1, YO, SSSK, K1, P2, slip marker, knit across to last 3 sts, K2 tog, K1: {54-54-58}{60-64-66} sts.

Row 11: K1, SSK, knit to marker, slip marker, P2, K3 tog, YO, K1, YO, K5, P2, K5, YO, K1, YO, SSSK, P2, slip marker, knit across to last 3 sts, K2 tog, K1: {52-52-56}{58-62-64} sts.

Row 13: K1, SSK, knit to marker, slip marker, P2, C8B, K1, P2, K1, C8F, P2, slip marker, knit across to last 3 sts, K2 tog, K1: {50-50-54}{56-60-62} sts.

Row 15: K1, SSK, knit to marker, slip marker, slip marker, P2, K5, K3 tog, YO, K1, YO, P2, YO, K1, YO, SSSK, K5, P2, slip marker, knit across to last 3 sts, K2 tog, K1: {48-48-52}{54-58-60} sts.

Repeat Rows 2 thru {11-11-13} {15-15-15} times: {38-38-40} {40-44-46} sts.

Size Large & 1X ONLY
Repeat Rows 2 and 3 once **more**: 38 sts.

Size 2X & 3X ONLY
Repeat Rows 2 thru {7-9} once **more**: 38 sts.

All Sizes
Next Row: P1, P2 tog, purl to marker, slip marker, K2, (P9, K2) twice, slip marker, purl across to last 3 sts, SSP, P1: 36 sts.

Sizes Large and 2X ONLY
Next Row: K1, SSK, knit to marker, slip marker, work across to marker, slip marker, knit across to last 3 sts, K2 tog, K1: 36 sts.

Bind off all sts in pattern.

FINISHING

Weave 3 of the 4 raglan seams *(Fig. 16, page 95)*.

Neckband

With **right** side facing, pick up {142-142-142}{146-146-146} sts evenly spaced along neck edge *(Figs. 13a & b, page 94)*.

Row 1 (Wrong side): Knit across.

Row 2: Purl across.

Row 3: Knit across.

Bind off all sts in **purl**.

Sew remaining raglan seam and Neckband, allowing Neckband to roll to the **wrong** side.

Weave underarm and side in one continuous seam.

Schematic Label	Description	Imperial Measurement / Metric Measurement
A	Chest Measurement	{36-39¼-42½}{44¾-48¾-52}" / {91.5-99.5-107.5}{114-124-132} cm
B	Hem to Underarm Length	16½" / 42 cm
C	Armhole Depth	{4½-4½-5}{5½-6-6½}" / {11.5-11.5-12.5}{14-15-16.5} cm
D	Neck Width	6" / 15 cm
E	Total Length Front and Back	{24½-24½-25}{25½-26-26½}" / {62-62-63}{64.5-66-67.5} cm
F	Sleeve Width at Lower Edge	{12½-12½-13¼}{13½-14½-14½}" / {31.5-31.5-33.5}{34.5-36.5-36.5} cm
G	Total Sleeve Length	{5½-5½-6}{6½-7-7½}" / {14-14-15}{16.5-18-19} cm
H	Sleeve Width at Neck Edge	6" / 15 cm

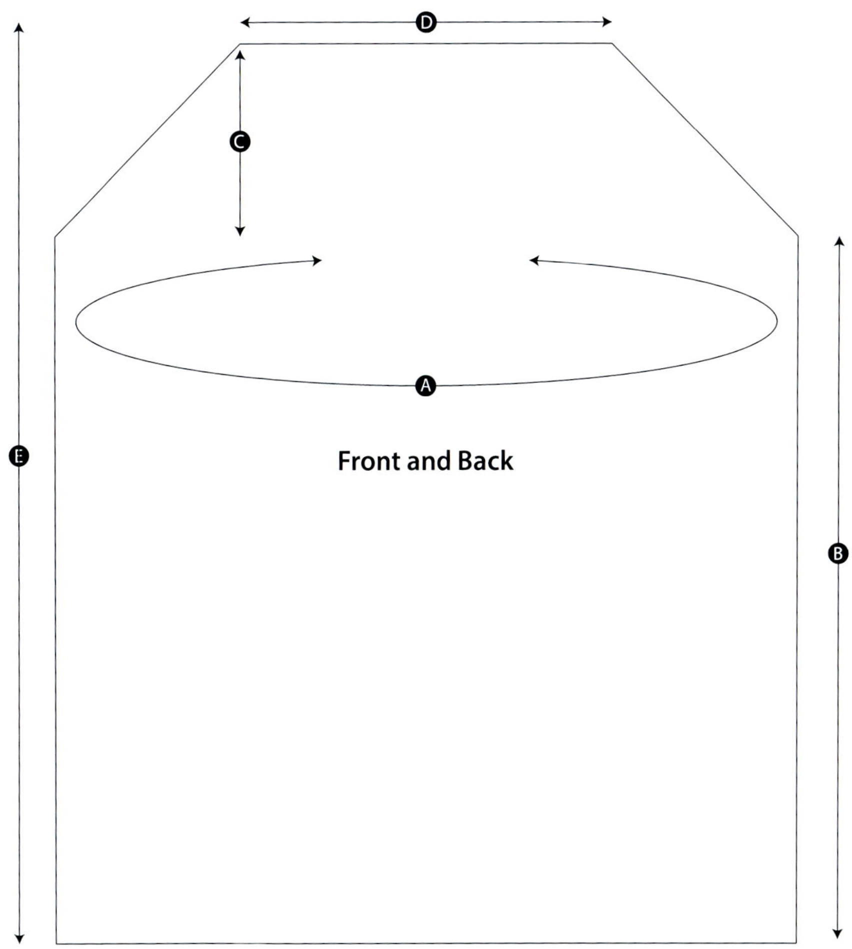

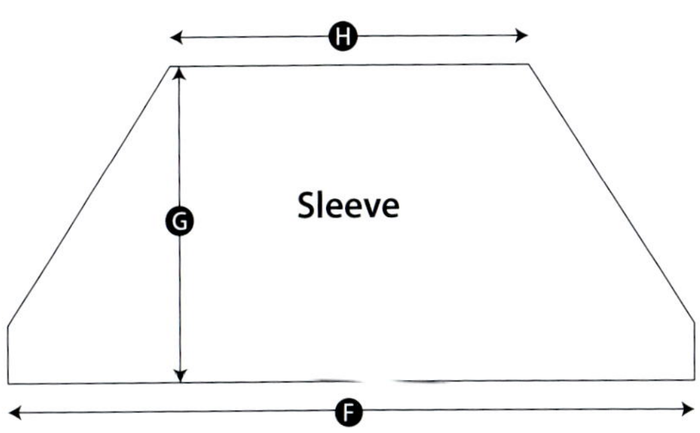

Scarf

●●○○ **EASY**

Finished Measurement:
7" wide x 78" long (18 cm x 198 cm), excluding fringe

SHOPPING LIST

Yarn (Bulky Weight) 5

[5 ounces, 132 yards
(141 grams, 121 meters) per skein]:

- ☐ 3 skeins

Knitting Needles

Straight,

- ☐ Size 10½ (6.5 mm) **or** size needed for gauge

Additional Supplies

- ☐ 12" (30.5 cm) scrap of cardboard (for winding fringe)
- ☐ Crochet hook (for attaching fringe)
- ☐ Yarn needle

GAUGE INFORMATION

In pattern, 15 sts and 16 rows = 4" (10 cm), blocked.

TECHNIQUES USED

- YO ***(Photo G, page 7)***
- K2 tog ***(Photo K, page 7)***
- SSK ***(Photo L & M, page 8)***
- YO twice ***(Fig. 7, page 93)***

SCARF

Cast on 26 sts.

Row 1 (RS)**:** K1, ★ K2 tog, YO twice, SSK; repeat from ★ across to last st, K1.

Note: When working into a double YO, knit in the first loop and purl in the second loop.

Row 2: (K3, P1) across to last 2 sts, K2.

Row 3: K1, YO, SSK, K2 tog, ★ YO twice, SSK, K2 tog; repeat from ★ across to last st, YO, K1.

Row 4: K5, P1, (K3, P1) across to last 4 sts, K4.

Repeat Rows 1-4 for pattern until Scarf measures approximately 78" (198 cm) from cast on edge, ending by working Row 3.

Bind off all sts in **knit**.

FINISHING

Wind yarn around 12" (30.5 cm) piece of cardboard 28 times. Attach 2 strands of fringe to each YO along the two short edges ***(Figs. 17a & b, page 95)***.

Trim fringe evenly.

CHART

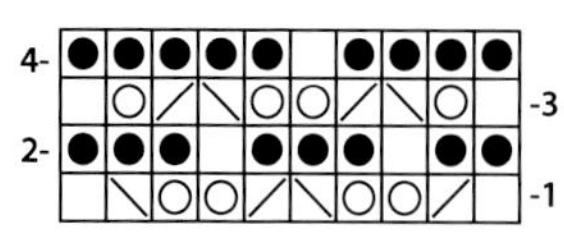

Repeat Rows 1-4 for pattern
Follow chart from right to left on RS rows;
follow chart from left to right on WS rows.

KEY

- ☐ knit on RS; purl on WS
- ● knit on WS
- ⧄ K2 tog
- ⧅ SSK
- ◯ YO

Baby Cardi

●●○○ EASY

SHOPPING LIST

Yarn (Medium Weight)

[7 ounces, 370 yards
(198 grams, 338 meters) per skein]:

☐ 1 skein

Knitting Needles

29" (73.5 cm) Circular,

☐ Size 8 (5 mm)
or size needed for gauge

Double-pointed needles (set of 5),

☐ Size 8 (5 mm) for Sleeves

Additional Supplies

☐ Stitch markers

☐ Scrap yarn (to use as st holders)

☐ Split ring marker

☐ 9/16" (14 mm) Buttons - 3

☐ Yarn needle

SIZE INFORMATION

Finished Chest Measurement:
21{23½-25}" / 53.5{59.5-63.5} cm

Size Note: For ease in following the pattern, we have printed the instructions for each size in a different color:

- Size 3-6 months in Blue
- Size 6-9 months in Pink
- Size 9-12 months in Green

GAUGE INFORMATION

In Stockinette Stitch,
16 sts and 20 rows = 4" (10 cm)

TECHNIQUES USED

- YO ***(Photo G, page 7)***
- K2 tog ***(Photo K, page 7)***
- SSK ***(Photos L & M, page 8)***
- Knit Increase ***(Figs. 3a & b, page 92)***

BODY

Neckband

Cast on 48{52-56} sts.

Rows 1 and 2: Knit across.

Row 3 (Right side - Buttonhole row)**:** Knit across to last 4 sts, [K2 tog, YO (buttonhole made)], K2.

Row 4: K4, place marker, knit increase across to last 4 sts, place marker, K4: 88{96-104} sts.

Yoke

Rows 1 and 2: Knit across.

Size 3-6 months ONLY

Row 3: K4, slip marker, ★ (K2, knit increase) twice, K3, knit increase; repeat from ★ to marker, slip marker, K4: 112 sts.

Size 6-9 months ONLY

Row 3: K4, slip marker, K1, knit increase, (K2, knit increase) 28 times, K1, knit increase, slip marker, K4: 126 sts.

Size 9-12 months ONLY

Row 3: K4, slip marker, (K2, knit increase) 32 times, slip marker, K4: 136 sts.

All Sizes

Row 4: Knit across, slipping markers.

Row 5: K4, slip marker, (K2 tog, YO) to marker, slip marker, K4.

Rows 6-8: K4, slip marker, purl to marker, slip marker, K4.

Row 9 (Buttonhole row)**:** Knit across to second marker, slip marker, [K2 tog, YO (buttonhole made)], K2.

Row 10: K4, slip marker, purl to marker, slip marker, K4.

Size 3-6 months ONLY

Row 11: K4, slip marker, ★ (K3, knit increase) twice, K4, knit increase; repeat from ★ to marker, slip marker, K4: 136 sts.

Size 6-9 months ONLY

Row 11: K4, slip marker, K2, knit increase, (K3, knit increase) 28 times, K2, knit increase, slip marker, K4: 156 sts.

Size 9-12 months ONLY

Row 11: K4, slip marker, (K3, knit increase) 32 times, slip marker, K4: 168 sts.

All Sizes

Row 12: Knit across, slipping markers.

Row 13: K4, slip marker, (K2 tog, YO) to marker, slip marker, K4.

Rows 14-16: K4, slip marker, purl to marker, slip marker, K4.

Row 17: Knit across, slipping markers.

Row 18: K4, slip marker, purl to marker, slip marker, K4.

Row 19 (Buttonhole row)**:** Knit across to second marker, slip marker, **[**K2 tog, YO (buttonhole made)**]**, K2.

Row 20: Knit across, slipping markers.

Row 21: K4, slip marker, (K2 tog, YO) to marker, slip marker, K4.

Rows 22-24: K4, slip marker, purl to marker, slip marker, K4.

Sizes 6-9 months and 9-12 months ONLY

Row 25: Knit across, slipping markers.

Row 26: K4, slip marker, purl to marker, slip marker, K4.

Size 9-12 months ONLY

Rows 27 and 28: Repeat Rows 25 and 26.

All Sizes

DIVIDE FOR LOWER BODY & SLEEVES

Row 1: K4, slip marker, knit 16{19-21} sts for left front, slip next 30{35-38} sts onto st holder for sleeve, **turn**; add on 4 sts for underarm ***(Figs. 8a & b, page 93)***, **turn**; knit 36{40-42} sts for back, slip next 30{35-38} sts to holder for sleeve, **turn**; add on 4 sts for underarm, **turn**; knit 20{23-25} sts for right front, slipping marker: 84{94-100} sts.

Row 2: K4, slip marker, purl to marker, slip marker, K4.

Row 3: Knit across, slipping markers.

Repeat Rows 2 and 3 until cardigan measures approximately 4¼{5¼-6¼}" / 11{13.5-16} cm from underarm or until ¾" (2 cm) less than desired finished length, ending by working a **right** side row and removing markers on last row.

Last 6 Rows: Knit across.

Bind off all sts in **knit**.

Sleeve

With **right** side facing and using double-pointed needles, pick up 4{3-4} sts across underarm ***(Figs. 13a & b, page 94)***, knit 30{35-38} sts from st holder: 34{38-42} sts.

Divide the stitches evenly onto four double-pointed needles *(see **Double-Pointed Needles, page 92**)*; place a split-ring marker to indicate the beginning of the round *(see **Markers, page 91**)*.

Work even in Stockinette Stitch until Sleeve measures approximately 3½{4½-5½}" / 9{11.5-14} cm from underarm.

CUFF

Rnd 1: Purl around.

Rnd 2: Knit around

Rnds 3-5: Repeat Rnds 1 and 2 once; then repeat Rnd 1 once **more**.

Bind off all sts in **knit**.

Repeat for second Sleeve.

FINISHING

Sew buttons opposite buttonholes.

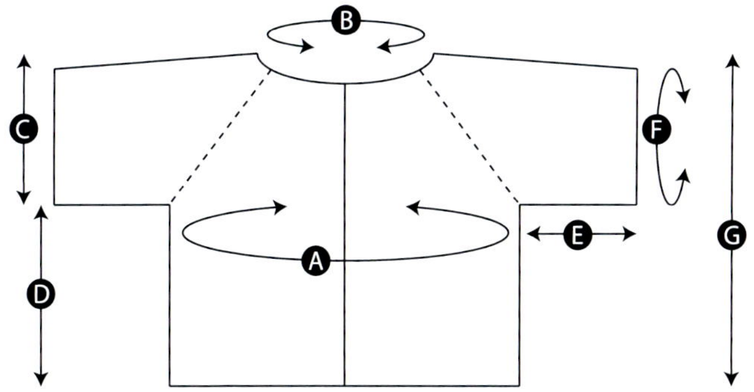

Schematic Label	Description	Imperial Measurement / Metric Measurement
A	Chest Measurement	21{23½-25}" / 53.5{59.5-63.5} cm
B	Neck Circumference	12{13-14}" / 30.5{33-35.5} cm
C	Armhole Depth	4¾{5¼-5½}" / 12{13.5-14} cm
D	Body Length to hem	5{6-7}" / 12.5{15-18} cm
E	Sleeve Length	4¼{5¼ 6¼}" / 11{13.5-16} cm
F	Sleeve Circumference	8½{9½-10½}" / 21.5{24-26.5} cm
G	Total Length	9¾{11¼-12½}" / 25{28.5-32} cm

Skinny Scarf

●●○○ EASY

Finished Size:
Approximately 3½" wide x 64" long (9 cm x 162.5 cm)

SHOPPING LIST

Yarn (Light Weight) 3 LIGHT

[3½ ounces, 232 yards (100 grams, 212 meters) per ball**]:**

☐ 1 ball

Knitting Needles

Straight,

☐ Size 6 (4 mm)

Additional Supplies

☐ Yarn needle

GAUGE INFORMATION

Gauge is not crucial for this project.

TECHNIQUES USED

- YO *(Photo G, page 7)*
- K2 tog *(Photo K, page 7)*
- SSK *(Photos L & M, page 8)*
- Knit Increase *(Figs. 3a & b, page 92)*

CHART

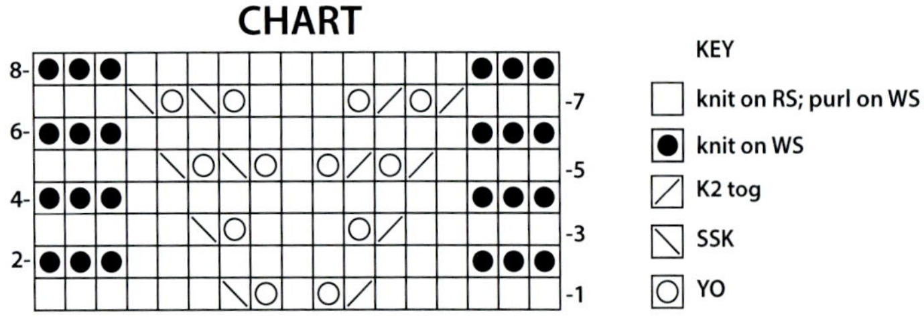

Repeat Rows 1-8 for pattern
Follow chart from right to left on RS rows; follow chart from left to right on WS rows.

Scarf

Cast on 16 sts.

Work in Garter Stitch (knit every row) for 6 rows, increasing one st evenly spaced across last row ***(see Increasing Evenly Across A Row, page 92)***: 17 sts.

Row 1 (Right side)**:** K6, K2 tog, YO, K1, YO, SSK, K6.

Row 2 AND ALL WRONG SIDE ROWS: K3, P 11, K3.

Row 3: K5, K2 tog, YO, K3, YO, SSK, K5.

Row 5: K4, (K2 tog, YO) twice, K1, (YO, SSK) twice, K4.

Row 7: K3, (K2 tog, YO) twice, K3, (YO, SSK) twice, K3.

Row 9: K6, K2 tog, YO, K1, YO, SSK, K6.

Repeat Rows 2-9 for pattern until Scarf measures approximately 62" (157.5 cm) from cast on edge, ending by working a **wrong** side row.

Next Row: Knit across decreasing one st evenly spaced: 16 sts.

Last 5 Rows: Knit across.

Bind off all sts in **knit**.

Block to finished measurements ***(see Blocking, page 9)***.

Bias Wrap

●●○○ **EASY**

Finished Size:
Approximately 78" wide x 20" deep (198 cm x 51 cm), blocked

SHOPPING LIST

Yarn (Medium Weight)

[3½ ounces, 218 yards (100 grams, 199 meters) per skein]:

- ☐ Pale Aqua - 6 skeins
- ☐ Medium Blue - 1 skein
- ☐ Teal - 1 skein

Knitting Needles

29" (73.5 cm) Circular,

- ☐ Size 10 (6 mm)
  or size needed for gauge

Additional Supplies

- ☐ Yarn needle

GAUGE INFORMATION

In pattern,
16 sts and 24 rows = 4" (10 cm), blocked.

TECHNIQUES USED

- YO ***(Photo G, page 7)***
- K2 tog ***(Photo K, page 7)***
- Knit S2KP2 ***(Photos N thru P, page 8)***
- Knit Increase ***(Figs. 3a & b, page 92)***
- Purl Increase ***(Fig. 4, page 93)***
- P2 tog ***(Fig. 10, page 94)***

COLOR SEQUENCE

4 rows of Medium Blue, ★ 23 rows of Pale Aqua, 5 rows of Teal, 23 rows of Pale Aqua, 5 rows of Medium Blue; repeat from ★ for stripe sequence.

WRAP

With Medium Blue, cast on 85 sts.

Row 1 (Right side)**:** Purl across.

Row 2: K1, K2 tog, knit across to last 2 sts, knit increase, K1.

Rows 3 and 4: Repeat Rows 1 and 2.

Row 5: With Pale Aqua, K4, ★ YO, K5, S2KP2, K5, YO; repeat from ★ once **more**, YO, K5, K2 tog, K4.

Row 6 AND ALL WRONG SIDE ROWS THRU ROW 26: P1, P2 tog, purl across to last 2 sts, purl increase, P1.

Row 7: Knit across.

Row 9: K6, ★ YO, K5, S2KP2, K5, YO, K1; repeat from ★ once **more**, YO, K5, K2 tog, K2.

Row 11: Knit across.

Row 13: K8, ★ YO, K5, S2KP2, K5, YO, K1; repeat from ★ once **more**, K7.

Row 15: Knit across.

Row 17: K2, K2 tog, K5, YO, K1, ★ YO, K5, S2KP2, K5, YO, K1; repeat from ★ once **more**, K5.

Row 19: Knit across.

Row 21: K4, K2 tog, K5, YO, K1, ★ YO, K5, S2KP2, K5, YO, K1; repeat from ★ once **more**, K3.

Row 23: Knit across.

Row 25: K6, K2 tog, K5, YO, K1, ★ YO, K5, S2KP2, K5, YO, K1; repeat from ★ once **more**, K1.

Row 27: Knit across.

Row 28: With next color, P1, P2 tog, purl across to last 2 sts, purl increase, P1.

Following Color Sequence, repeat Rows 1-28 for pattern until Wrap measures approximately 78" (198 cm) from cast on edge, ending by working Row 3.

Bind off all sts in **knit**.

Block to finished measurements ***(see Blocking, page 9)***.

CHART

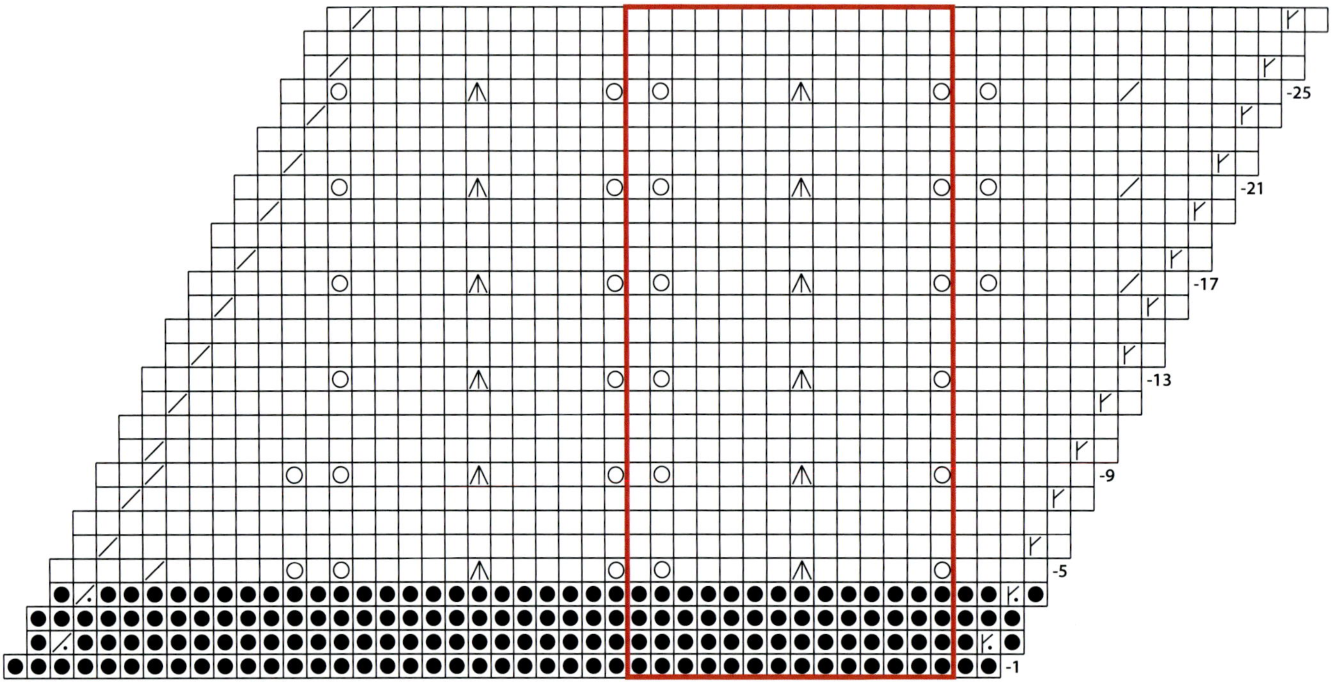

KEY

- knit on RS; purl on WS
- purl on RS; knit on WS
- K2 tog on RS; P2 tog on WS
- K2 tog on WS
- Knit Increase
- Purl Increase
- YO
- S2KP2
- pattern repeat

Repeat Rows 1-28 for pattern

Follow chart from right to left on RS rows; follow chart from left to right on WS rows.

Two-Color Shawl

●●○○ **EASY**

Finished Size:

Approximately 70" wide x 40" deep (178 cm x 101.5 cm), blocked

SHOPPING LIST

Yarn (Fine Weight) 2

[3½ ounces, 326 yards (100 grams, 295 meters) per skein**]:**

- ☐ Color A (Gray) - 3 skeins
- ☐ Color B (Rose) - 2 skeins

Knitting Needles

29" (73.5 cm) Circular,

- ☐ Size 5 (3.75 mm)
  or size needed for gauge

Double-pointed,

- ☐ Size 5 (3.75 mm)

Additional Supplies

- ☐ Crochet hook size E (3.5 mm) (for provisional cast on)
- ☐ Scrap yarn
- ☐ Stitch markers
- ☐ Yarn needle

GAUGE INFORMATION

In Stockinette Stitch,
24 sts and 28 rows = 4" (10 cm), blocked.

TECHNIQUES USED

- YO ***(Photos G & J, page 7)***
- K2 tog ***(Photo K, page 7)***
- SSK ***(Photos L & M, page 8)***
- SSSK ***(see Decreases, page 8)***
- S2KP2 ***(Photos N thru P, page 8)***
- P2 tog ***(Fig. 10, page 94)***

SHAWL

Garter Tab

With the scrap yarn, work provisional cast on as follows: With crochet hook, ch 7. Cut the yarn and pull the end through the last chain made to secure it. Tie a loose knot on this tail to mark it as the end you'll use later to unravel the chain.

Working in back ridge of crocheted chain ***(Fig. 14, page 95)*** and using knitting needle and Color A, pick up one st in each of center 3 chs: 3 sts.

Rows 1-7: Knit across.

Rotate piece 90°; pick up 3 sts across side edge ***(Figs. 13a&b, page 94)***; rotate piece 90° again; unzip provisional cast on, with second needle pick up 3 live stitches across provisional cast on edge and knit them: 9 sts.

Row 8 (Right side)**:** Purl across.

Row 9: K3, P3, K3.

First Lace Section

Row 1 (RS): K3, place marker, YO, K1, YO, place marker, K1, place marker, YO, K1, YO, place marker, K3: 13 sts.

Row 2 AND ALL WRONG SIDE ROWS: K3, slip marker, purl across to last marker slipping markers at center, slip last marker, K3.

Row 3: K3, slip marker, YO, K3, YO, slip marker, K1, slip marker, YO, K3, YO, slip marker, K3: 17 sts.

Row 5: K3, slip marker, YO, K1, YO, SSSK, YO, K1, YO, slip marker, K1, slip marker, YO, K1, YO, SSSK, YO, K1, YO, slip marker, K3: 21 sts.

Row 7: K3, slip marker, YO, K2, YO, SSSK, YO, K2, YO, slip marker, K1, slip marker, YO, K2, YO, SSSK, YO, K2, YO, slip marker, K3: 25 sts.

Row 9: K3, slip marker, YO, K3, YO, SSSK, YO, K3, YO, slip marker, K1, slip marker, YO, K3, YO, SSSK, YO, K3, YO, slip marker, K3: 29 sts.

Row 11: K3, slip marker, YO, K4, YO, SSSK, YO, K4, YO, slip marker, K1, slip marker, YO, K4, YO, SSSK, YO, K4, YO, slip marker, K3: 33 sts.

Row 13: K3, † slip marker, YO, SSK, YO, K3, (YO, SSSK, YO, K3) to within 2 sts of marker, YO, SSK, YO, slip marker †, K1, repeat from † to † once, K3: 37 sts.

Row 15: K3, † slip marker, YO, K1, SSK, YO, K3, (YO, SSSK, YO, K3) to within 3 sts of marker, YO, SSK, K1, YO, slip marker †, K1, repeat from † to † once, K3: 41 sts.

Row 17: K3, † slip marker, YO, K1, (YO, SSSK, YO, K3) to within 4 sts of marker, YO, SSSK, YO, K1, YO, slip marker †, K1, repeat from † to † once, K3: 45 sts.

Row 19: K3, † slip marker, YO, K2, (YO, SSSK, YO, K3) to within 5 sts of marker, YO, SSSK, YO, K2, YO, slip marker †, K1, repeat from † to † once, K3: 49 sts.

Row 21: K3, † slip marker, YO, K3, (YO, SSSK, YO, K3) to marker, YO, slip marker †, K1, repeat from † to † once, K3: 53 sts.

Row 23: K3, † slip marker, YO, K4, (YO, SSSK, YO, K3) to within one st of marker, K1, YO, slip marker †, K1, repeat from † to † once, K3: 57 sts.

Rows 25-108: Repeat Rows 13-24, 7 times: 225 sts.

Cut Color A.

FIRST LACE SECTION

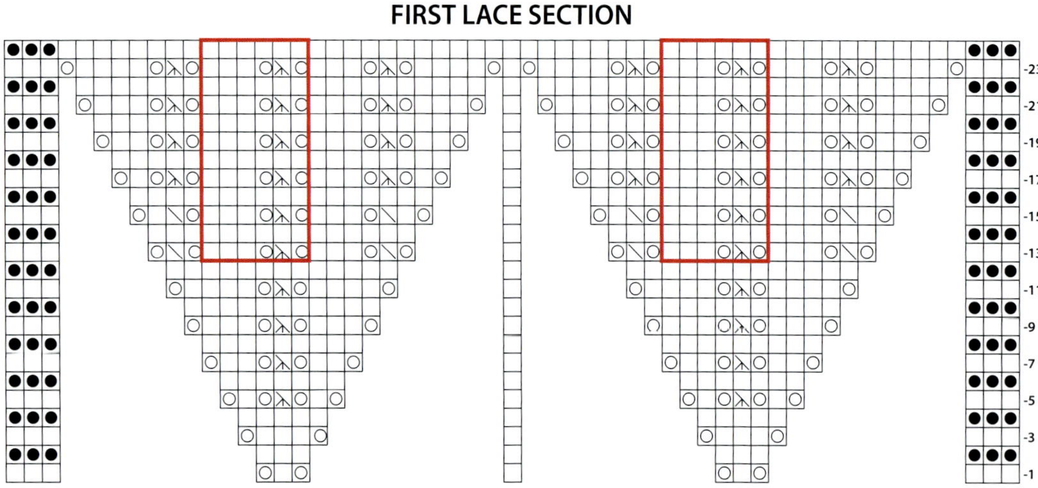

KEY

- knit on RS; purl on WS
- knit on WS
- YO
- SSSK
- SSK
- pattern repeat

Work Rows 1-28, then repeat Rows 13-24 for pattern.
Follow chart from right to left on RS rows;
follow chart from left to right on WS rows.

SECOND LACE SECTION

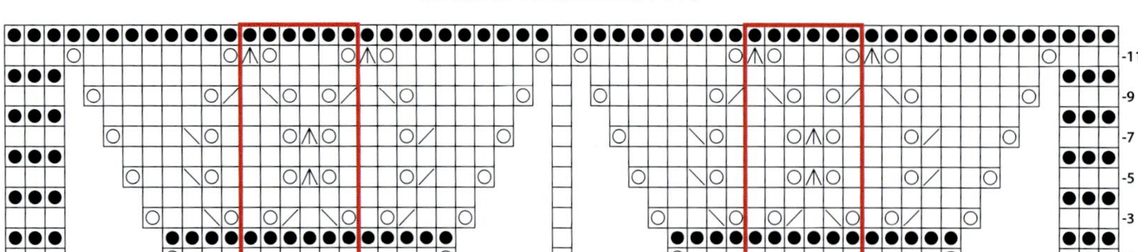

KEY

- knit on RS; purl on WS
- knit on WS
- YO
- S2KP2
- SSK
- K2 tog
- pattern repeat

Work Rows 1-12 for pattern.
Follow chart from right to left on RS rows;
follow chart from left to right on WS rows..

Second Lace Section

Row 1 (RS)**:** With Color B, K3, † slip marker, YO, knit to marker, YO, slip marker †, K1, repeat from † to † once, K3: 229 sts.

Row 2: (Knit to marker, slip marker) twice, P1, slip marker, knit to marker, slip marker, K3.

Row 3: K3, † slip marker, YO, K2, K2 tog, YO, K1, (YO, SSK, K1, K2 tog, YO, K1) to within 4 sts of marker, YO, SSK, K2, YO, slip marker †, K1, repeat from † to † once, K3: 233 sts.

Row 4 AND ALL WRONG SIDE ROWS THRU ROW 10: K3, slip marker, purl across to last marker slipping markers at center, slip last marker, K3.

Row 5: K3, † slip marker, YO, K2, K2 tog, YO, K3, YO, (SK2P2, YO, K3, YO) to within 4 sts of marker, SSK, K2, YO, slip marker †, K1, repeat from † to † once, K3: 237 sts.

Row 7: K3, † slip marker, YO, K3, K2 tog, YO, K2, (K1, YO, SK2P2, YO, K2) to within 6 sts of marker, K1, YO, SSK, K3, YO, slip marker †, K1, repeat from † to † once, K3: 241 sts.

Row 9: K3, † slip marker, YO, K5, YO, SSK, K1, (K2 tog, YO, K1, YO, SSK, K1) to within 7 sts of marker, K2 tog, YO, K5, YO, slip marker †, K1, repeat from † to † once, K3: 245 sts.

Row 11: K3, † slip marker, YO, K7, YO, SK2P2, (YO, K3, YO, SK2P2) to within 7 sts of marker, YO, K7, YO, slip marker †, K1, repeat from † to † once, K3: 249 sts.

Row 12: (Knit to marker, slip marker) twice, P1, slip marker, knit to marker, slip marker, K3.

Cut Color B.

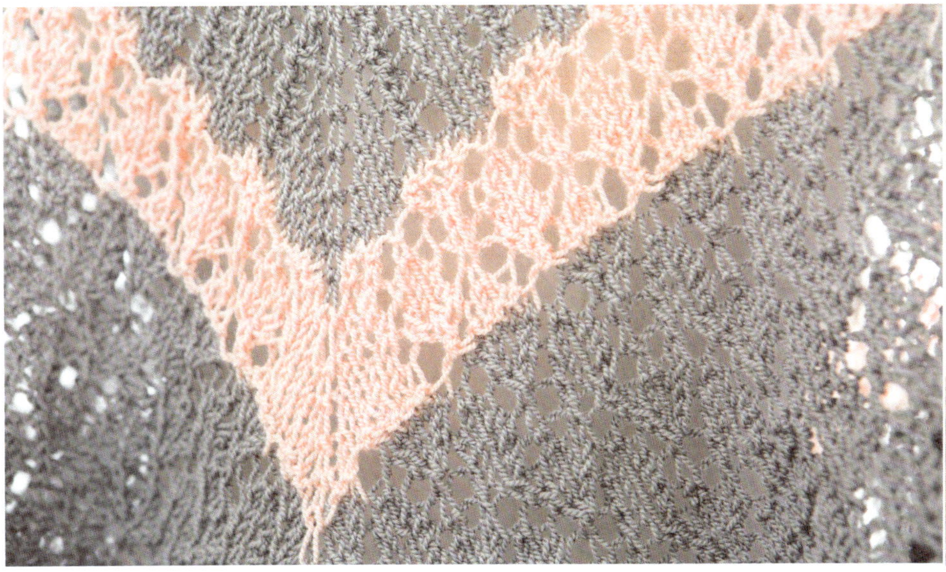

THIRD LACE SECTION

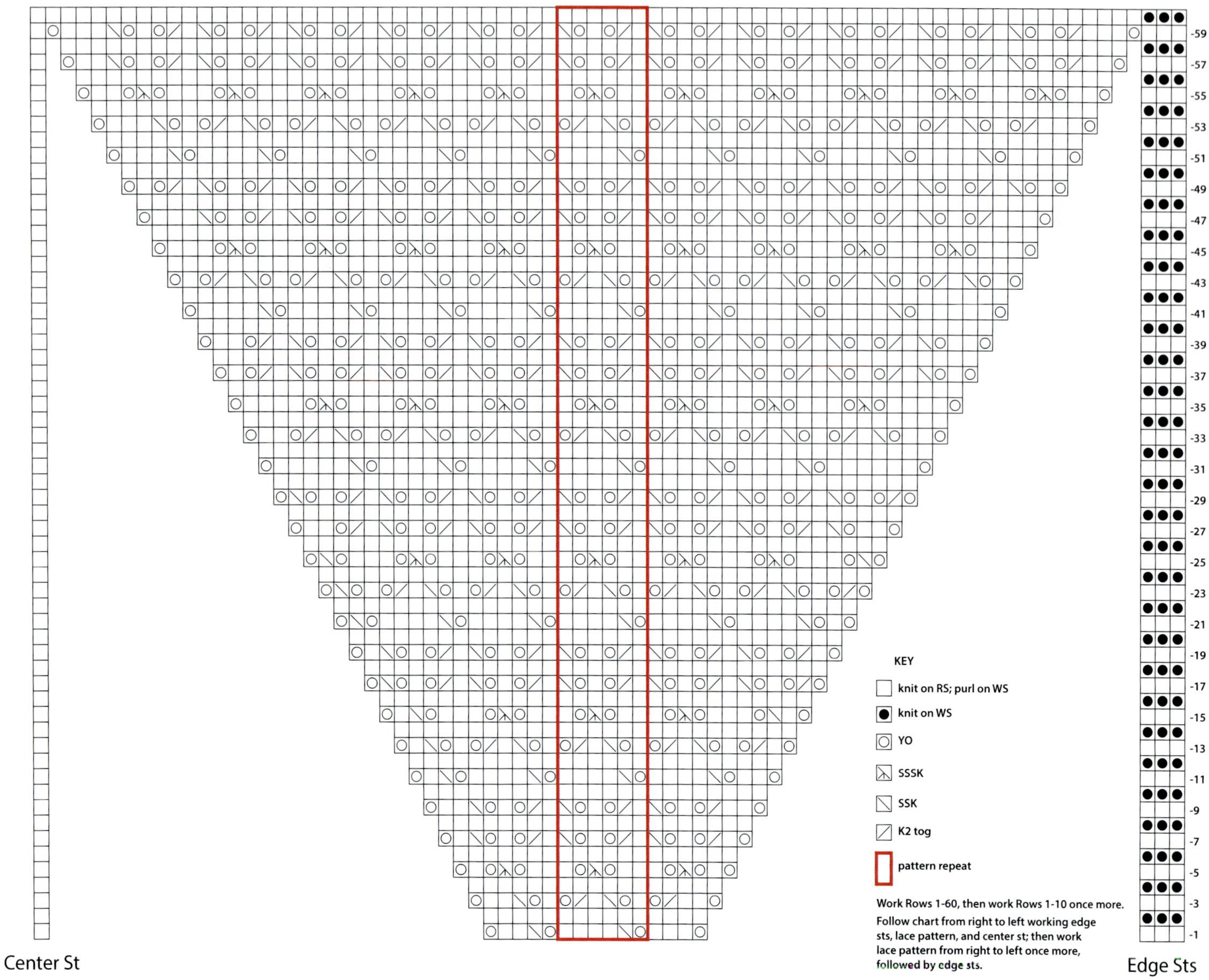

Third Lace Section

Row 1: With Color A, K3, † slip marker, YO, K3, (YO, SSK, K4) to within 4 sts of marker, YO, SSK, K2, YO, slip marker †, K1, repeat from † to † once, K3: 253 sts.

Row 2 AND ALL WRONG SIDE ROWS: K3, slip marker, purl across to last marker slipping markers at center, slip last marker, K3.

Row 3: K3, † slip marker, YO, K2, K2 tog, YO, (K1, YO, SSK, K1, K2 tog, YO) to within 5 sts of marker, K1, YO, SSK, K2, YO, slip marker †, K1, repeat from † to † once, K3: 257 sts.

Row 5: K3, † slip marker, YO, K1, YO, SSSK, YO, K1, (K2, YO, SSSK, YO, K1) to marker, YO, slip marker †, K1, repeat from † to † once, K3: 261 sts.

Row 7: K3, † slip marker, YO, (K1, K2 tog, YO, K1, YO, SSK) to within one st of marker, K1, YO, slip marker †, K1, repeat from † to † once, K3: 265 sts.

Row 9: K3, † slip marker, YO, K2, K2 tog, YO, K1, YO, SSK, (K1, K2 tog, YO, K1, YO, SSK) to within 2 sts of marker, K2, YO, slip marker †, K1, repeat from † to † once, K3: 269 sts.

Row 11: K3, † slip marker, (YO, K2, YO, SSK, K4) to within 3 sts of marker, YO, SSK, K1, YO, slip marker †, K1, repeat from † to † once, K3: 273 sts.

Row 13: K3, † slip marker, YO, K1, K2 tog, YO, (K1, YO, SSK, K1, K2 tog, YO) to within 4 sts of marker, K1, YO, SSK, K1, YO, slip marker †, K1, repeat from † to † once, K3: 277 sts.

Row 15: K3, † slip marker, YO, K1, SSK, YO, K1, (K2, YO, SSSK, YO, K1) to within 5 sts of marker, K2, YO, SSK, K1, YO, slip marker †, K1, repeat from † to † once, K3: 281 sts.

Row 17: K3, † slip marker, YO, K2 tog, YO, K1, YO, SSK, (K1, K2 tog, YO, K1, YO, SSK) to marker, YO, slip marker †, K1, repeat from † to † once, K3: 285 sts.

Row 19: K3, † slip marker, YO, (K1, K2 tog, YO, K1, YO, SSK) to within one st of marker, K1, YO, slip marker †, K1, repeat from † to † once, K3: 289 sts.

Row 21: K3, † slip marker, YO, K1, (YO, SSK, K4) to within 2 sts of marker, YO, SSK, YO, slip marker †, K1, repeat from † to † once, K3: 293 sts.

Row 23: K3, † slip marker, YO, K2 tog, YO, (K1, YO, SSK, K1, K2 tog, YO) to within 3 sts of marker, K1, YO, SSK, YO, slip marker †, K1, repeat from † to † once, K3: 297 sts.

Row 25: K3, † slip marker, YO, SSK, YO, K1, (K2, YO, SSSK, YO, K1) to within 4 sts of marker, K2, YO, SSK, YO, slip marker †, K1, repeat from † to † once, K3: 301 sts.

Row 27: K3, † slip marker, YO, K2, YO, SSK, (K1, K2 tog, YO, K1, YO, SSK) to within 5 sts of marker, K1, K2 tog, YO, K2, YO, slip marker †, K1, repeat from † to † once, K3: 305 sts.

Row 29: K3, † slip marker, YO, K2 tog, YO, K1, YO, SSK, (K1, K2 tog, YO, K1, YO, SSK) to marker, YO, slip marker †, K1, repeat from † to † once, K3: 309 sts.

Row 31: K3, † slip marker, YO, K6, (YO, SSK, K4) to within one st of marker, K1, YO, slip marker †, K1, repeat from † to † once, K3: 313 sts.

Row 33: K3, † slip marker, YO, K1, (K1, YO, SSK, K1, K2 tog, YO) to within 2 sts of marker, K2, YO, slip marker †, K1, repeat from † to † once, K3: 317 sts.

Row 35: K3, † slip marker, YO, K2, (K2, YO, SSSK, YO, K1) to within 3 sts of marker, K3, YO, slip marker †, K1, repeat from † to † once, K3: 321 sts.

Row 37: K3, † slip marker, YO, K1, YO, SSK, (K1, K2 tog, YO, K1, YO, SSK) to within 4 sts of marker, K1, K2 tog, YO, K1, YO, slip marker †, K1, repeat from † to † once, K3: 325 sts.

Row 39: K3, † slip marker, YO, K2, YO, SSK, (K1, K2 tog, YO, K1, YO, SSK) to within 5 sts of marker, K1, K2 tog, YO, K2, YO, slip marker †, K1, repeat from † to † once, K3: 329 sts.

Row 41: K3, † slip marker, YO, K5, (YO, SSK, K4) across to marker, YO, slip marker †, K1, repeat from † to † once, K3: 333 sts.

Row 43: K3, † slip marker, YO, (K1, YO, SSK, K1, K2 tog, YO) to within one st of marker, K1, YO, slip marker †, K1, repeat from † to † once, K3: 337 sts.

Row 45: K3, † slip marker, YO, K1, (K2, YO, SSSK, YO, K1) to within 2 sts of marker, K2, YO, slip marker †, K1, repeat from † to † once, K3: 341 sts.

Row 47: K3, † slip marker, YO, K2, (K1, K2 tog, YO, K1, YO, SSK) to within 3 sts of marker, K3, YO, slip marker †, K1, repeat from † to † once, K3: 345 sts.

Row 49: K3, † slip marker, YO, K1, YO, SSK, (K1, K2 tog, YO, K1, YO, SSK) to within 4 sts of marker, K1, K2 tog, YO, K1, YO, slip marker †, K1, repeat from † to † once, K3: 349 sts.

Row 51: K3, † slip marker, YO, K4, (YO, SSK, K4) to within 5 sts of marker, YO, SSK, K3, YO, slip marker †, K1, repeat from † to † once, K3: 353 sts.

Row 53: K3, † slip marker, YO, K3, K2 tog, YO, (K1, YO, SSK, K1, K2 tog, YO) to within 6 sts of marker, K1, YO, SSK, K3, YO, slip marker †, K1, repeat from † to † once, K3: 357 sts.

Row 55: K3, † slip marker, YO, (K2, YO, SSSK, YO, K1) to within one st of marker, K1, YO, slip marker †, K1, repeat from † to † once, K3: 361 sts.

Row 57: K3, † slip marker, YO, K1, (K1, K2 tog, YO, K1, YO, SSK) to within 2 sts of marker, K2, YO, slip marker †, K1, repeat from † to † once, K3: 365 sts.

Row 59: K3, † slip marker, YO, K2, (K1, K2 tog, YO, K1, YO, SSK) to within 3 sts of marker, K3, YO, slip marker †, K1, repeat from † to † once, K3: 369 sts.

Rows 61-70: Repeat Rows 1-10: 389 sts.

Cut Color A.

Edging

With Color B and using double-pointed needle, cast on 11 sts.

Row 1 (Right side)**:** Slip 1 as if to **knit**, K3, YO, SSK, YO, K2 tog, YO, K3.

Row 2: K3, P5, YO, P2 tog, P1, slip next st as if to **knit**, knit next st from body of shawl, PSSO.

Row 3: Slip 1 as if to **knit**, K3, YO, SSK, YO, K2 tog, YO, K4.

Row 4: Bind off first 2 sts (one st remaining on right needle), K3, P3, YO, P2 tog, P1, slip next st as if to **knit**, knit next st from body of shawl, PSSO.

Repeat Rows 1-4 across body of shawl, ending by working Row 3.

Bind off sts loosely in **purl**.

EDGING

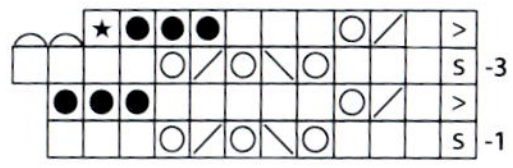

KEY

- S slip 1 as if to knit
- knit on RS; purl on WS
- knit on WS
- YO
- SSK
- K2 tog on RS rows; P2 tog on WS rows
- > Joining st: Slip st as if to knit, K1 from shawl body, PSSO
- ★ St on right needle after bind off
- Bind off

Work Rows 1-4 for pattern.
Follow chart from right to left on RS rows; follow chart from left to right on WS rows.

Lace-Border Top

●●○○ **EASY**

SHOPPING LIST

Yarn (Light Weight) LIGHT 3

[3½ ounces, 232 yards

(100 grams, 212 meters) per ball]:

☐ {4-5-6}{7-8-9} balls

Knitting Needles

Straight,

☐ Size 6 (4 mm)

or size needed for gauge

Additional Supplies

☐ Open ring stitch markers - 4

☐ Yarn needle

SIZE INFORMATION

Finished Chest Measurement:

{36¼-40¾-45¼}{50-54½-59}" /

{92-103.5-115}{127-138.5-150} cm

Finished Length: 24" (61 cm)

Size Note: For ease in following the pattern, we have printed the instructions for each size in a different color:

- Size Small in Blue
- Size Medium in Pink
- Size Large in Green
- Size 1X in Red
- Size 2X in Purple
- Size 3X in Orange

GAUGE INFORMATION

In Stockinette Stitch,

21 sts and 28 rows = 4" (10 cm),

blocked.

TECHNIQUES USED

- YO *(Photo J, page 07)*
- P2 tog *(Fig. 10, page 94)*

BACK

Cast on {97-109-121}{133-145-157} sts.

Row 1 (Right side)**:** K1, (P3, K1) across.

Row 2: P1, (K3, P1) across.

Rows 3 and 4: Repeat Rows 1 and 2.

Row 5: K1, (P2 tog, YO, P1, K1) across.

Row 6: P1, (K3, P1) across.

CHART

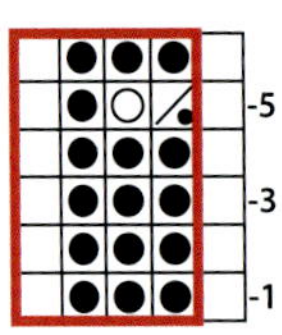

KEY

☐ knit on RS; purl on WS

● purl on RS; knit on WS

○ YO

P2 tog

pattern repeat

Repeat Rows 1-6 for pattern.

Follow chart from right to left on RS rows; follow chart from left to right on WS rows.

Repeat Rows 1-6 for pattern until piece measures approximately 4" (10 cm) from the cast on edge, ending by working a **wrong** side row.

Next 4 Rows: Knit across.

Work in Stockinette Stitch until piece measures approximately 18¾" (47.5 cm) from cast on edge, ending by working a **wrong** side row.

Next 4 Rows: Knit across.

Repeat Rows 1-6 until piece measures 24" (61 cm) from cast on edge, ending by working a **right** side row.

Bind off all sts **loosely** in pattern.

FRONT

Work same as Back.

FINISHING

Sew shoulder seams, leaving center 9½" (24 cm) open for neck.

Place markers on each side of Front and Back {7-7½-8}{8½-9-9}"/ {18-19-20.5}{21.5-23-24} cm down from shoulder seam.

Armband

With **right** side facing, pick up {75-79-83}{87-91-95} sts between markers *(Figs. 13a & b, page 94)*.

Row 1: Purl across.

Row 2: Knit across.

Row3: Purl across.

Bind off all sts in **knit**.

Repeat for second Armband.

Weave each Armband and side in one continuous seam *(Fig. 16, page 95)*, ending 4" (10 cm) from cast on edge.

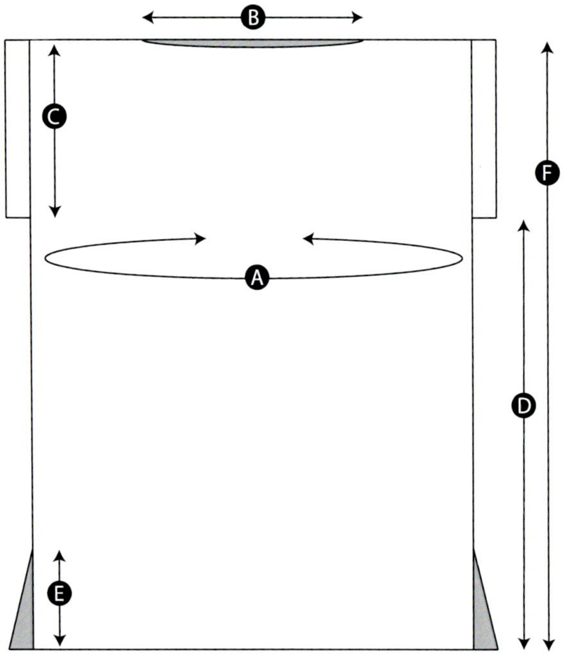

Schematic Label	Description	Imperial Measurement / Metric Measurement
A	Chest Measurement	{36¼-40¾-45¼}{50-54½-59}" / {92-103.5-115}{127-138.5-150} cm
B	Neck Width	9½" / 24 cm
C	Armhole Depth	{7-7½-8}{8½-9-9}" / {18-19-20.5}{21.5-23-23} cm
D	Body Length to hem	{17-16½-16}{15½-15-15}" / {43-42-40.5}{39.5-38-38} cm
E	Lower Vent Opening	4" / 10 cm
F	Total Length	24" / 61 cm

Long Vest

●●○○ EASY

SHOPPING LIST

Yarn (Medium Weight)

[16 ounces, 867 yards
(454 grams, 792 meters) per skein]:

☐ 1{2-2-2} skeins

Knitting Needles

29" (73.5 cm) Circular,

☐ Size 8 (5 mm) **or** size needed for gauge

Additional Supplies

☐ Yarn needle

SIZE INFORMATION

Finished Chest Measurement:
39{46-55½-64½}" / 99{117-141-164} cm

Finished Length: 29" (73.5 cm)

Size Note: For ease in following the pattern, we have printed the instructions for each size in a different color:

- Size Small/Medium in Blue
- Size Large in Pink
- Size 1X/2X in Green
- Size 3X in Red

GAUGE INFORMATION

In Stockinette Stitch,
15 sts and 17 rows = 4" (10 cm), blocked

In Lace Pattern,
14 sts and 18 rows = 4" (10 cm), blocked

STITCH GUIDE

BOBBLE (uses one st)

Knit into the (front, back, front) of **next** st, **turn**; P1, (P1, YO, P1) **all** in next st, P1, **turn**; K5, turn; P2 tog, P1, P2 tog, **turn**; SK2P2.

TECHNIQUES USED

- YO ***(Photo G, page 7)***
- K2 tog ***(Photo K, page 7)***
- SSK ***(Photos L & M, page 8)***
- S2KP2 ***(Photos N thru P, page 8)***
- P2 tog ***(Fig. 10, page 94)***
- SSP ***(Fig. 12, page 94)***

BACK

Cast on 65{81-97-113} sts.

Foundation Row 1 (Right side)**:** K8, work Bobble, (K7, work Bobble) across to last 8 sts, K8: 7{9-11-13} Bobbles.

Foundation Row 2: Knit across.

Lower Band

Row 1: K2 tog, K2, YO, K1, YO, K2, ★ SK2P2, K2, YO, K1, YO, K2; repeat from ★ across to last 2 sts, SSK.

Row 2: Knit across.

Repeat Rows 1 and 2 until piece measures approximately 2" (5 cm) from cast on edge, ending by working a **wrong** side row.

Body

Row 1 (Right side)**:** K2, K2 tog, YO, ★ K1, YO, SSK, K3, K2 tog, YO; repeat from ★ across to last 5 sts, K1, YO, SSK, K2.

Row 2 AND ALL WRONG SIDE ROWS: Purl across.

Row 3: K1, K2 tog, YO, K1, ★ YO, SSK, K1, K2 tog, YO, K1; repeat from ★ across to last 5 sts, K2, YO, SSK, K1.

LOWER BAND

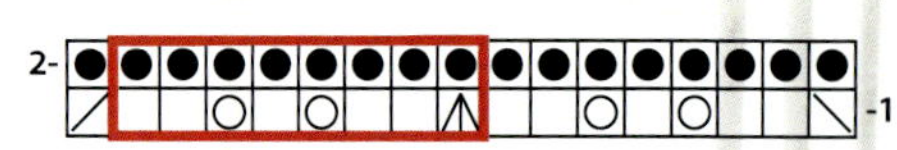

KEY

- knit on RS; purl on WS
- knit on WS
- K2 tog
- SSK
- YO
- S2KP2
- pattern repeat

Work Rows 1and 2 for pattern.

Follow chart from right to left on RS rows; follow chart from left to right on WS rows.

Row 5: K2 tog, YO, K2, ★ K3, YO, SK2P2, YO, K2; repeat from ★ across to last 5 sts, K3, YO, SSK.

Rows 7-10: Repeat Rows 5 and 6 twice.

Row 11: K2, YO, SSK, ★ K1, K2 tog, YO, K3, YO, SSK; repeat from ★ across to last 5 sts, K1, K2 tog, YO, K2.

Row 13: K3, YO, ★ SK2P2, YO, K5, YO; repeat from ★ across to last 6 sts, SK2P2, YO, K3.

Row 15: K1, YO, SSK, K1, ★ K2, K2 tog, YO, K1, YO SSK, K1; repeat from ★ across to last 5 sts, K2, K2 tog, YO, K1.

Row 17: Repeat Row 11.

Rows 19-24: Repeat Rows 13 and 14, 3 times.

Rows 25-28: Repeat Rows 3-6.

Repeat Rows 1-28 for pattern until Back measures approximately 16{15½-15-14½}"/40.5{39.5-38-37} cm from cast on edge, ending by working Row 14 or Row 28.

Next Row: Knit across increasing 4{6-8-8} sts evenly spaced ***(see Increasing Evenly Across A Row, page 92)***: 69{87-105-121} sts.

Next Row: Knit across.

Work in Stockinette Stitch until Back measures approximately 20{19½-19-18½}"/51{49.5-48.5-47} cm from cast on edge, ending by working a **purl** row.

ARMHOLE SHAPING

Rows 1 and 2: Bind off 4{6-8-10} sts, work across: 61{75-89-101} sts.

Rows 3 and 4: Bind off 2{4-6-8} sts, work across: 57{67-77-85} sts.

Row 5 (Decrease row)**:** SSK, knit across to last 2 sts, K2 tog: 55{65-75-83} sts.

Row 6 (Decrease row)**:** P2 tog, purl across to last 2 sts, SSP: 53{63-73-81} sts.

Sizes Large-1X/2X-3X ONLY

Repeat Rows 5 and 6, {2-3-4} times: {55-61-65} sts.

All Sizes

Next Row (Decrease row)**:** SSK, knit across to last 2 sts, K2 tog: 51{53-59-63} sts.

Next Row: Purl across.

Repeat last 2 rows, 3{2-1-1} time(s): 45{49-57-61} sts.

Work even until Back measures approximately 27½" (70 cm) from cast on edge, ending by working a **purl** row.

BODY PATTERN

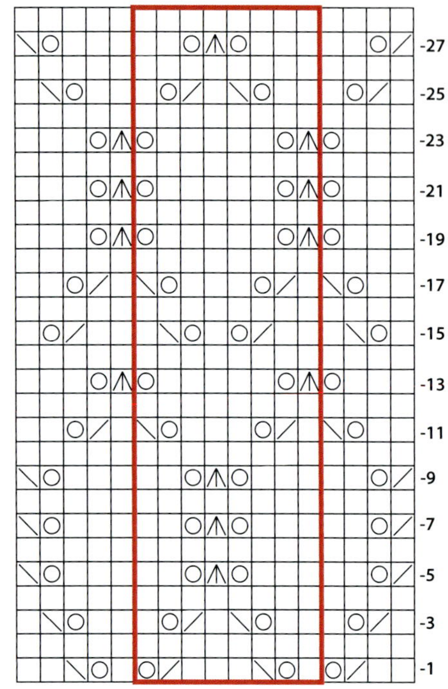

KEY

knit on RS; purl on WS

K2 tog

SSK

YO

S2KP2

pattern repeat

Work Rows 1-28 for pattern.

Follow chart from right to left on RS rows; follow chart from left to right on WS rows.

NECK SHAPING

Note: Both sides of neck are worked at the same time, using separate yarn for each side.

Row 1: Knit 11{13-17-19} sts; with second yarn, bind off next 23 sts, knit across: 11{13-17-19} sts **each** side.

Row 2: Purl across to within 2 sts of Neck edge, SSP; with second yarn, P2 tog, purl across: 10{12-16-18} sts **each** side.

Work even until Back measures approximately 28" (71 cm) from cast on edge, ending by working a **purl** row.

SHOULDER SHAPING

Row 1: Bind off 5{6-8-9} sts, knit across; with second yarn, knit across.

Row 2: Bind off 5{6-8-9} sts, purl across; with second yarn, purl across: 5{6-8-9} sts **each** side.

Row 3: Bind off sts to Neck edge; with second yarn, knit across.

Row 4: Bind off remaining sts.

LEFT FRONT

Cast on 33{41-49-57} sts.

Work same as Back until Left Front measures approximately 16{15½-15-14½}"/40.5{39.5-38-37} cm from cast on edge, ending by working Row 14 or Row 28.

Next Row: Knit across increasing 3{3-3-4} sts evenly spaced: 36{44-52-61} sts.

Next Row: Knit across.

Work in Stockinette Stitch until Left Front measures approximately 20{19½-19-18½)"/51{49.5-48.5-47} cm from cast on edge, ending by working a **purl** row.

ARMHOLE SHAPING

Row 1: Bind off 4{6-8-10} sts, knit across: 32{38-44-51} sts.

Row 2: Purl across.

Row 3: Bind off 2{4-6-8} sts, knit across: 30{34-38-43} sts.

Row 4: Purl across to last 2 sts, SSP: 29{33-37-42} sts.

Row 5: SSK, knit across: 28{32-36-41} sts.

Sizes Large-1X/2X-3X ONLY

Repeat Rows 4 and 5, {2-3-4} times: {28-30-33} sts.

All Sizes

Next Row: Purl across.

Next Row (Decrease row)**:** SSK, knit across: 27{27-29-32} sts.

Repeat last 2 rows, 3{2-1-1} time(s): 24{25-28-31} sts.

Work even until Left Front measures approximately 26" (66 cm) from cast on edge, ending by working a **knit** row.

NECK SHAPING

Row 1: Bind off 6{5-4-5) sts, purl across: 18{20-24-26} sts.

Row 2: Knit across.

Row 3: Bind off 3 sts, purl across: 15{17-21-23} sts.

Row 4: Knit across.

Row 5: Bind off 2 sts, purl across: 13{15-19-21} sts.

Row 6: Knit across to last 2 sts, K2 tog: 12{14-18-20} sts.

Row 7: P2 tog, purl across: 11{13-17-19} sts.

Row 8: Knit across to last 2 sts, K2 tog: 10{12-16-18} sts.

Work even until Left Front measures same as Back to shoulders, ending by working a **purl** row.

SHOULDER SHAPING

Row 1: Bind off 5{6-8-9} sts, knit across: 5{6-8-9} sts.

Row 2: Purl across.

Bind off remaining sts.

RIGHT FRONT

Work same as Left Front to Armhole Shaping, ending by working a **knit** row: 36{44-52-61} sts.

ARMHOLE SHAPING

Row 1: Bind off 4{6-8-10} sts, purl across: 32{38-44-51} sts.

Row 2: Knit across.

Row 3: Bind off 2{4-6-8} sts, purl across: 30{34-38-43} sts.

Row 4: Knit across to last 2 sts, K2 tog: 29{33-37-42} sts.

Row 5: P2 tog, purl across: 28{32-36-41} sts.

Sizes Large-1X/2X-3X ONLY

Repeat Rows 4 and 5, {2-3-4} times: {28-30-33} sts.

All Sizes

Next Row: Knit across to last 2 sts, K2 tog: 27{27-29-32} sts.

Next Row: Purl across.

Repeat last 2 rows, 3{2-1-1} time(s): 24{25-28-31} sts.

Work even until Right Front measures approximately 26" (66 cm) from cast on edge, ending by working a **purl** row.

NECK SHAPING

Row 1: Bind off 6{45-4-5} sts, knit across: 18{20-24-26} sts.

Row 2: Purl across.

Row 3: Bind off 3 sts, knit across: 15{17-21-23} sts.

Row 4: Purl across.

Row 5: Bind off 2 sts, knit across: 13{15-19-21} sts.

Row 6: Purl across to last 2 sts, SSP: 12{14-18-20} sts.

Row 7: SSK, knit across: 11{13-17-19} sts.

Row 8: Purl across to last 2 sts, SSP: 10{12-16-18} sts.

Work even until Right Front measures same as Back to Shoulder Shaping, ending by working a **knit** row.

SHOULDER SHAPING

Row 1: Bind off 5{6-8-9} sts, purl across: 5{6-8-9} sts.

Row 2: Knit across.

Bind off remaining sts.

FINISHING

Sew shoulder seams.

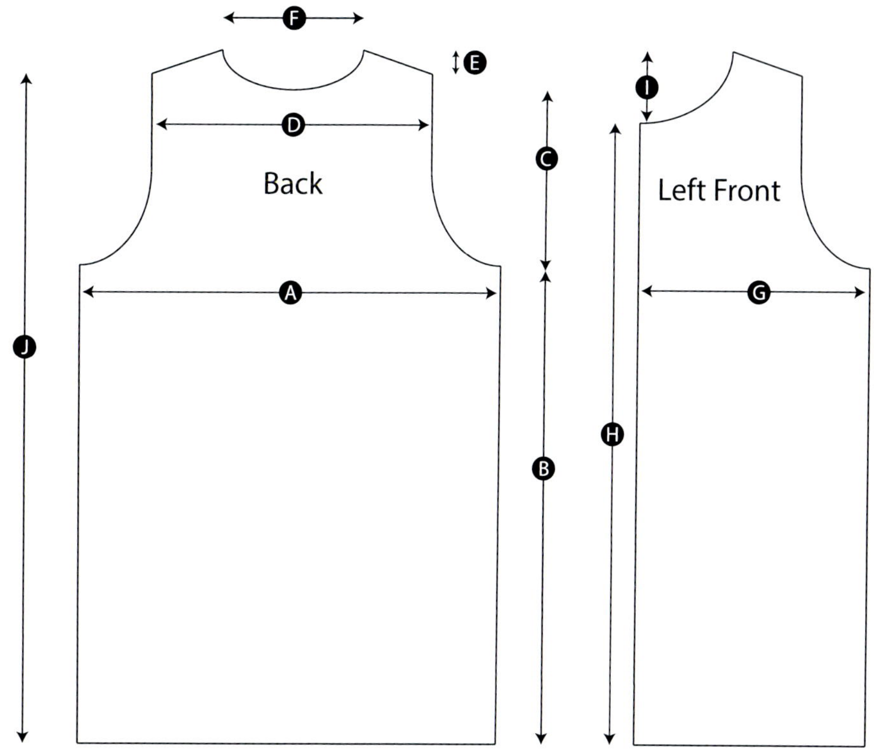

Neck Edging

With **right** side facing, pick up 82 sts along neck edge ***(Figs. 13a & b, page 94)***.

Work in Garter Stitch for ½" (12 mm).

Next Row: Knit across decreasing 8 sts evenly spaced: 74 sts.

Work even until Neck Edging measures 1" (2.5 cm).

Bind off all sts.

Front Edging

With **right** side facing, pick up 115 sts evenly spaced along Left Front edge.

Work in Garter Stitch for 1" (2.5 cm).

Bind off all sts.

Repeat for second side.

Armhole Edging

With **right** side facing, pick up 74{78-82-86} sts along armhole edge.

Work in Garter Stitch for 1" (2.5 cm).

Bind off all sts.

Repeat for second armhole.

Weave side seams ***(Fig. 16, page 95)***.

Schematic Label	Description	Imperial Measurement / Metric Measurement
A	Width across Back	18½{23-27¾-32¼}" / 47{58.5-70.5-82} cm
B	Hem to Underarm Length	20{19½-19-18½}" / 51{49.5-48.5-47} cm
C	Armhole Depth to Neck Shaping	8{8½-9-9½}" / 20.5{21.5-23-24} cm
D	Width across Shoulders	11½{12½-14¾-15¾}" / 29{32-37.5-40} cm
E	Shoulder Shaping	1" / 2.5 cm
F	Neck Width	6¾" / 17 cm
G	Left Front Width	9{11¼-13¼-15¾}" / 23{28.5-33.5-40} cm
H	Left Front Length to Neck Shaping	26" / 66 cm
I	Front Neck Depth	3" / 7.5 cm
J	Total Length	29" / 73.5 cm

Assymetrical Wrap

●●○○ **EASY**

Finished Measurement:
42" wide x 69" long
(106.5 cm x 175.5 cm)

SHOPPING LIST

Yarn (Light Weight) (3 LIGHT)

[3½ ounces, 437 yards
(100 grams, 400 meters) per ball**]**:

☐ 1 ball

Knitting Needles

29" (73.5 cm) Circular,

☐ Size 10½ (6.5 mm)

or size needed for gauge

Additional Supplies

☐ Yarn needle

GAUGE INFORMATION

In pattern,
16 sts and 16 rows = 4" (10 cm),
blocked.

TECHNIQUES USED

- YO ***(Photos G & J, page 7)***
- K2 tog ***(Photo K, page 7)***
- SSK ***(Photos N thru P, page 8)***
- K3 tog ***(Fig. 11, page 94)***

WRAP

Cast on one st.

Row 1 (Right side): (K1, YO, K1) **all** in first st: 3 sts.

Row 2: P1, YO, P2: 4 sts.

Row 3: K3, YO, K1: 5 sts.

Row 4: P1, YO, P4: 6 sts.

Row 5: K5, YO, K1: 7 sts.

Row 6: P1, YO, P6: 8 sts.

Row 7: K7, YO, K1: 9 sts.

Row 8: P1, YO, P8: 10 sts.

Row 9: K9, YO, K1: 11 sts.

Row 10: P1, YO, P 10: 12 sts.

Row 11: K 11, YO, K1: 13 sts.

Row 12: Purl across.

Row 13: K2 tog, K2, YO, SSK, K1, K2 tog, YO, K3, YO, K1.

Row 14 AND ALL WRONG SIDE ROWS: P1, YO, purl across: 14 sts.

Note: Each **wrong** side row adds one st. The stitch count remains the same on the following **right** side row.

Row 15: K2 tog, K3, K2 tog, YO, K6, YO, K1.

Row 17: K2 tog, K1, K2 tog, YO, K6, K2 tog, (YO, K1) twice: 15 sts.

Row 19: K2 tog, K7, K2 tog, YO, K4, YO, K1: 16 sts.

Row 21: K2 tog, K2, YO, SSK, K1, K2 tog, YO, K3, YO, SSK, K2, YO, K1: 17 sts.

Row 23: K2 tog, K2, YO, SSK, K6, YO, SSK, K3, YO, K1: 18 sts.

Row 25: K2 tog, K2, YO, SSK, K6, YO, SSK, K4, YO, K1: 19 sts.

Row 27: K2 tog, K2, YO, SSK, K6, YO, SSK, K5, YO, K1: 20 sts.

Row 29: K2 tog, K2, ★ YO, SSK, K1, K2 tog, YO, K3; repeat from ★ across to last st, YO, K1: 21 sts.

Row 31: K2 tog, K1, ★ K2, K2 tog, YO, K4; repeat from ★ across to last 3 sts, K2, YO, K1: 22 sts.

Row 33: K2 tog, ★ K1, K2 tog, YO, K5; repeat from ★ across to last 5 sts, K1, K2 tog, (YO, K1) twice: 23 sts.

Row 35: K3 tog, YO, K6, ★ K2 tog, YO, K6; repeat from ★ across to last 7 sts, K2 tog, YO, K4, YO, K1: 24 sts.

Row 37: K2 tog, K2, YO, SSK, K1, K2 tog, ★ YO, K3, YO, SSK, K1, K2 tog; repeat from ★ across to last 8 sts, YO, K3, YO, SSK, K2, YO, K1: 25 sts.

Row 39: K2 tog, K2, YO, SSK, K1, ★ K5, YO, SSK, K1; repeat from ★ across to last 43 sts, K2, YO, K1: 26 sts.

Row 41: K2 tog, K2, YO, SSK, ★ K6, YO, SSK; repeat from ★ across to last 5 sts, K4, YO, K1: 27 sts.

Row 43: K2 tog, K2, YO, ★ SSK, K6, YO; repeat from ★ across to last 8 sts, SSK, K5, YO, K1: 28 sts.

Rows 45-236: Repeat Rows 29-44, 12 times: 125 sts.

Bind off all sts loosely in **knit**.

CHART

Work Rows 1-44, then repeat Rows 29-44 for pattern.

Follow chart from right to left on RS rows; follow chart from left to right on WS rows.

Sampler Cardigan

●●○○ **EASY**

SHOPPING LIST

Yarn (Medium Weight) MEDIUM 4

[3½ ounces, 198 yards

(100 grams, 181 meters) per skein]:

☐ {8-10-11}{12-13-14} balls

Knitting Needles

29" (73.5 cm) Circular,

☐ Size 8 (5 mm)

or size needed for gauge

Additional Supplies

☐ Split ring marker - 4

☐ Yarn needle

SIZE INFORMATION

Finished Chest Measurement:

{38-43-47½}{52½-57-62}"/

{96.5-109-120.5}{133.5-145-157.5} cm

Finished Length: 29" (73.5 cm)

Size Note: For ease in following the pattern, we have printed the instructions for each size in a different color:

- Size Small in Blue
- Size Medium in Pink
- Size Large in Green
- Size 1X in Red
- Size 2X in Purple
- Size 3X in Orange

GAUGE INFORMATION

In Stockinette Stitch,

20 sts and 24 rows = 4" (10 cm)

TECHNIQUES USED

- YO ***(Photo G, page 7)***
- K2 tog ***(Photo K, page 7)***
- SSK ***(Photos L & M, page 8)***
- M1 ***(Figs. 5a & b, page 93)***
- M1P ***(Figs. 6a & b, page 93)***

BACK

Border

Cast on {96-108-120}{132-144-156} sts.

Rows 1-4: (K3, P3) across.

Rows 5-8: (P3, K3) across.

Repeat Rows 1-8 until piece measures approximately 4" (10 cm) from cast on edge, ending by working Row 4 or Row 8 and increasing one st on last row: {97-109-121}{133-145-157} sts.

BORDER

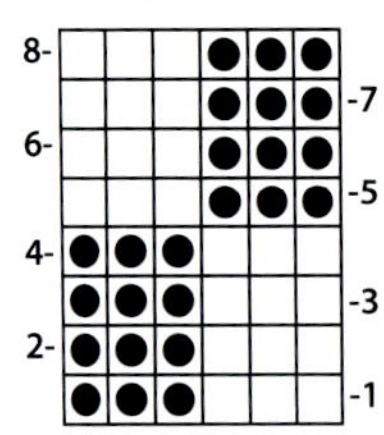

KEY

☐ knit on RS; purl on WS

● knit on WS; purl on RS

Repeat Rows 1-8 for pattern.

Follow chart from right to left on RS rows; follow chart from left to right on WS rows.

First Garter Ridge

Rows 1-4: Knit across.

Beginning with a **knit** row, work in Stockinette Stitch until piece measures approximately 13" (33 cm) from cast on edge, ending by working a **purl** row.

Second Garter Ridge

Rows 1-4: Knit across.

First Lace Section

Row 1 (Right side)**:** P3, K2 tog, K1, (YO, K1) twice, SSK, ★ P5, K2 tog, K1, (YO, K1) twice, SSK; repeat from ★ across to last 3 sts, P3.

Row 2: K3, P7, (K5, P7) across to last 3 sts, K3.

Row 3: P2, K2 tog, K1, YO, K3, YO, K1, SSK, ★ P3, K2 tog, K1, YO, K3, YO, K1, SSK; repeat from ★ across to last 2 sts, P2.

Row 4: K2, P9, (K3, P9) across to last 2 sts, K2.

Row 5: P1, ★ K2 tog, K1, YO, K5, YO K1, SSK, P1; repeat from ★ across.

Row 6: K1, (P 11, K1) across.

Row 7: P1, (K 11, P1) across.

Row 8: P3, K7, (P5, K7) across to last 3 sts, P3.

Row 9: K1, YO, K1, SSK, P5, K2 tog, ★ K1, (YO, K1) twice, SSK, P5, K2 tog; repeat from ★ across to last 2 sts, K1, YO, K1.

Row 10: P4, K5, (P7, K5) across to last 4 sts, P4.

Row 11: K2, YO, K1, SSK, P3, K2 tog, K1, ★ YO, K3, YO, K1, SSK, P3, K2 tog, K1; repeat from ★ across to last 2 sts, YO, K2.

Row 12: P5, K3, (P9, K3) across to last 5 sts, P5.

Row 13: K3, YO, K1, SSK, P1, K2 tog, K1, ★ YO, K5, YO, K1, SSK, P1, K2 tog, K1; repeat from ★ across to last 3 sts, YO, K3.

Row 14: P6, K1, (P 11, K1) across to last 6 sts, P6.

Row 15: K6, P1, (K 11, P1) across to last 6 sts, K6.

Row 16: K4, P5, (K7, P5) across to last 4 sts, K4.

Repeat Rows 1-16 until piece measures approximately 23" (58.5 cm) from cast on edge, ending by working a **wrong** side row.

Third Garter Ridge

Rows 1-4: Knit across.

FIRST LACE SECTION
BACK - ALL SIZES
LEFT FRONT - SIZES MEDIUM, 1X AND 3X
RIGHT FRONT - SIZES MEDIUM, 1X AND 3X

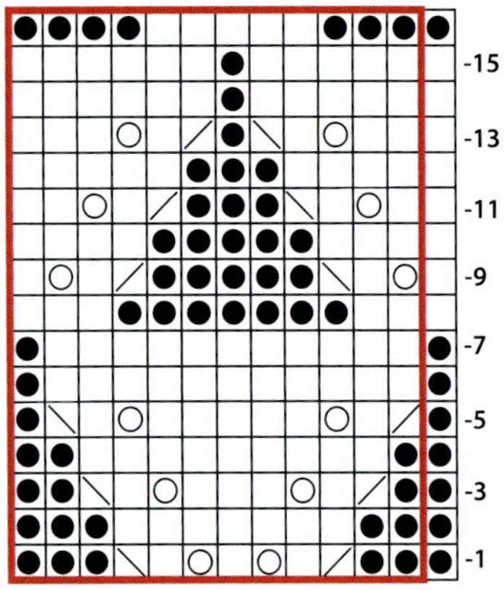

KEY

- knit on RS; purl on WS
- knit on WS; purl on RS
- K2 tog
- SSK
- YO
- pattern repeat

Repeat Rows 1-16 for pattern.

Follow chart from right to left on RS rows; follow chart from left to right on WS rows.

Second Lace Section

Row 1: K1, ★ YO, SSK, K1, K2 tog, YO, K1; repeat from ★ across.

Row 2: Purl across.

Repeat Rows 1 and 2 until piece measures approximately 29" (73.5 cm) from cast on edge, ending by working a **purl** row.

Bind off all sts in **knit**.

SECOND LACE SECTION

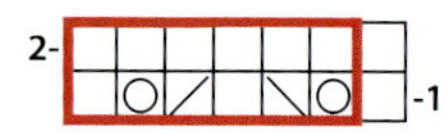

KEY

- knit on RS; purl on WS
- K2 tog
- SSK
- YO
- pattern repeat

Repeat Rows 1and 2 for pattern.

Follow chart from right to left on RS rows; follow chart from left to right on WS rows.

LEFT FRONT

Border

Cast on {30-36-42}{48-54-60} sts.

Work same as Back: {31-37-43}{49-55-61} sts.

Sizes Medium, 1X, and 3X ONLY

Complete same as Back, beginning at First Garter Ridge.

Sizes Small, Large, and 2X ONLY

Work same as Back to First Lace Section.

First Lace Section

Row 1: K1, YO, K1, SSK, ★ P5, K2 tog, K1, (YO, K1) twice, SSK; repeat from ★ across to last 3 sts, P3.

Row 2: K3, (P7, K5) across to last 4 sts, P4.

Row 3: K2, YO, K1, SSK, ★ P3, K2 tog, K1, YO, K3, YO, K1, SSK; repeat from ★ across to last 2 sts, P2.

Row 4: K2, (P9, K3) across to last 5 sts, P5.

Row 5: K3, YO, K1, SSK, P1, ★ K2 tog, K1, YO, K5, YO, K1, SSK, P1; repeat from ★ across.

Row 6: K1, (P 11, K1) across to last 6 sts, P6.

Row 7: K6, P1, (K 11, P1) across.

Row 8: P3, (K7, P5) across to last 4 sts, K4.

Row 9: P3, K2 tog, K1, ★ (YO, K1) twice, SSK, P5, K2 tog, K1; repeat from ★ across to last st, YO, K1.

Row 10: P4, (K5, P7) across to last 3 sts, K3.

Row 11: P2, K2 tog, K1, YO, ★ K3, YO, K1, SSK, P3, K2 tog, K1; repeat from ★ across to last 2 sts, YO, K2.

Row 12: P5, (K3, P9) across to last 2 sts, K2.

Row 13: P1, K2 tog, K1, ★ YO, K5, YO, K1, SSK, P1, K2 tog, K1; repeat from ★ across to last 3 sts, YO, K3.

Row 14: P6, K1, (P 11, K1) across.

Row 15: P1, (K 11, P1) across to last 6 sts, K6.

Row 16: K4, (P5, K7) across to last 3 sts, K3.

Repeat Rows 1-16 until piece measures approximately 23" (58.5 cm) from cast on edge, ending by working a **wrong** side row.

Complete same as Back, beginning with Third Garter Ridge.

FIRST LACE SECTION
LEFT FRONT - SIZES SMALL, LARGE, AND 2X

KEY

- knit on RS; purl on WS
- knit on WS; purl on RS
- K2 tog
- SSK
- YO
- pattern repeat

Repeat Rows 1-16 for pattern.

Follow chart from right to left on RS rows; follow chart from left to right on WS rows.

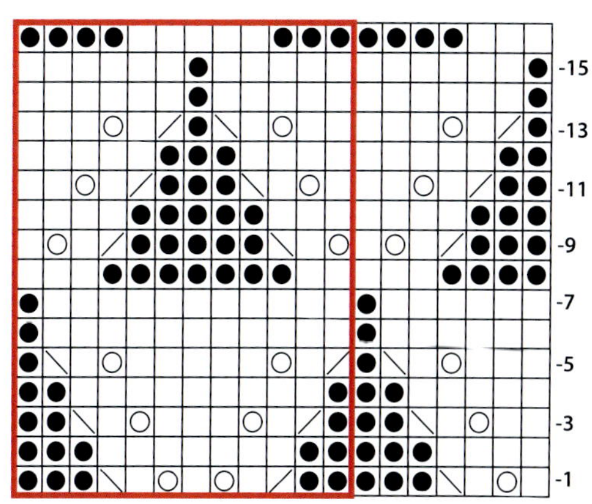

RIGHT FRONT

Sizes Medium, 1X, and 3X ONLY

Work same as Left Front.

Sizes Small, Large, and 2X ONLY

Work same as Left Front to First Lace Section.

First Lace Section

Row 1 (Right side)**:** P3, K2 tog, K1, ★ (YO, K1) twice, SSK, P5, K2 tog, K1; repeat from ★ across to last st, YO, K1.

Row 2: P4, (K5, P7) across to last 3 sts, K3.

Row 3: P2, K2 tog, K1, ★ YO, K3, YO, K1, SSK, P3, K2 tog, K1; repeat from ★ across to last 2 sts, YO, K2.

Row 4: P5, (K3, P9) across to last 2 sts, K2.

Row 5: P1, K2 tog, K1, ★ YO, K5, YO, K1, SSK, P1, K2 tog, K1; repeat from ★ across to last 3 sts, YO, K3.

Row 6: P6, K1, (P 11, K1) across.

Row 7: P1, (K 11, P1) across to last 6 sts, K6.

Row 8: K4, (P5, K7) across to last 3 sts, P3.

Row 9: K1, YO, K1, SSK, ★ P5, K2 tog, K1, (YO, K1) twice, SSK; repeat from ★ across to last 3 sts, P3.

Row 10: K3, (P7, K5) across to last 4 sts, P4.

Row 11: K2, YO, K1, SSK, ★ P3, K2 tog, K1, YO, K3, YO, K1, SSK; repeat from ★ across to last 2 sts, P2.

Row 12: K2, (P9, K3) across to last 5 sts, P5.

Row 13: K3, YO, K1, SSK, P1, ★ K2 tog, K1, YO, K5, YO, K1, SSK, P1; repeat from ★ across.

Row 14: K1, (P 11, K1) across to last 6 sts, P6.

Row 15: K6, P1, (K 11, P1) across.

Row 16: P3, (K7, P5) across to last 4 sts, K4.

Repeat Rows 1-16 until piece measures approximately 23" (58.5 cm) from cast on edge, ending by working a **wrong** side row.

FIRST LACE SECTION
RIGHT FRONT - SIZES SMALL, LARGE, AND 2X

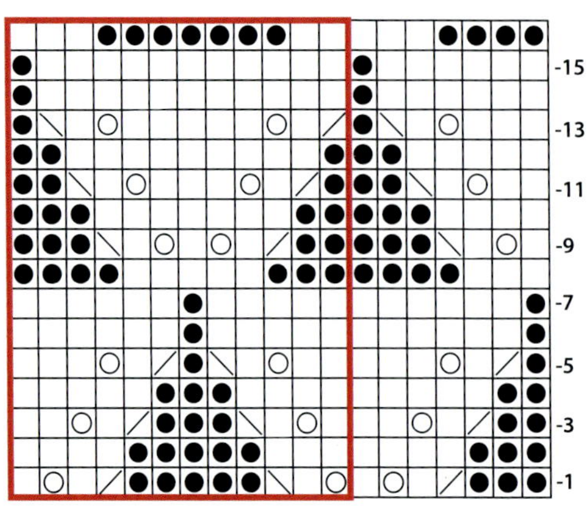

KEY

- knit on RS; purl on WS
- knit on WS; purl on RS
- K2 tog
- SSK
- YO
- pattern repeat

Repeat Rows 1-16 for pattern.

Follow chart from right to left on RS rows; follow chart from left to right on WS rows.

Complete same as Back, beginning with Third Garter Ridge.

SLEEVE (Make 2)

Cast on 42 sts.

Rows 1 and 2: (K3, P3) across.

Sizes Small and Medium ONLY

Rows 3 and 4: Repeat Rows 1 and 2.

Row 5: K1, M1P, P2, (K3, P3) across to last 3 sts, K2, M1, P1: 44 sts.

Rows 6-8: K1, (P3, K3) across to last st, P1.

Row 9: P1, M1P, (K3, P3) across to last st, M1, K1: 46 sts.

Rows 10-16: Maintaining pattern, continue to increase one st at each edge in same manner, every 4 rows once **more**: 48 sts.

Sizes Large, 1X, 2X and 3X ONLY

Row 3 (Increase row)**:** K1, M1, K2, (P3, K3) across to last 3 sts, P2, M1P, P1: 44 sts.

Row 4: P1, (K3, P3) across to last st, K1.

Row 5: K1, M1, (P3, K3) across to last st, M1P, P1: 46 sts.

Row 6: K2, (P3, K3) across to last 2 sts, P2.

Size Large ONLY

Rows 7 and 8: Repeat Row 6 twice.

Row 9: P1, M1P, P1, (K3, P3) across to last 2 sts, K1, M1, K1: 48 sts.

Rows 10-16: Maintaining pattern, continue to increase one st in same manner at each edge, every 4 rows once **more**: 50 sts.

Size 1X ONLY

Rows 7-14: Maintaining pattern, continue to increase one st in same manner at each edge, every other row, 4 times **more**: 54 sts.

Rows 15 and 16: Work across in established pattern.

Sizes 2X and 3X ONLY

Rows 7-16: Maintaining pattern, continue to increase one st in same manner at each edge, every other row, 5 times **more**: 56 sts.

All Sizes

Beginning with a **knit** row and working in Stockinette Stitch, continue to increase one st at each edge in same manner, every {4-4-4}{4-2-2} rows, {5-8-18}{16-5-8} times **more**: {58-64-86}{86-66-72} sts.

Sizes Small, Medium, 2X, and 3X ONLY

Continue working in Stockinette Stitch, increasing every {6-6}{4-4} rows, {11-8}{12-9} times: {80-80}{90-90} sts.

All Sizes

Work even until Sleeve measures approximately {19-18¼-17}{15¾-15-14}"/{48.5-46.5-43}{40-38-35.5} cm from cast on edge, ending by working a **purl** row.

Bind off all sts in **knit**.

FINISHING

Sew shoulder seams.

Neck & Front Band

With **right** side facing and beginning at lower Right Front, pick up 363 sts evenly spaced along Right Front, Back neck, and Left Front *(Figs. 13a & b, page 94)*.

Row 1 (WS)**:** K3, (P3, K3) across.

Row 2: P3, (K3, P3) across.

Row 3: K3, (P3, K3) across.

Rows 4 and 5: P3, (K3, P3) across.

Rows 6-8: Repeat Rows 1-3.

Repeat Rows 1-8 until Band measures 8" (20.5 cm), ending by working Row 4 or Row 8.

Bind off all sts in pattern.

FRONT BAND

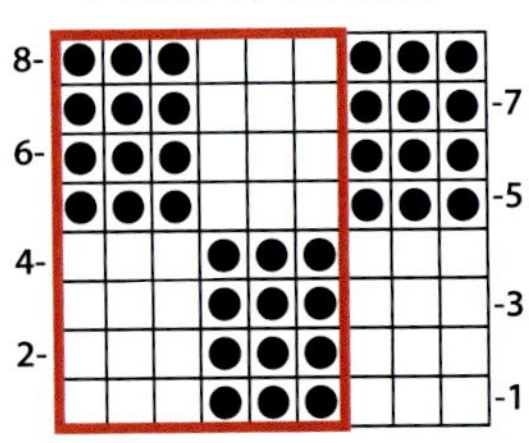

KEY

☐ knit on RS; purl on WS

● knit on WS; purl on RS

▯ pattern repeat

Repeat Rows 1-8 for pattern.

Follow chart from right to left on RS rows; follow chart from left to right on WS rows.

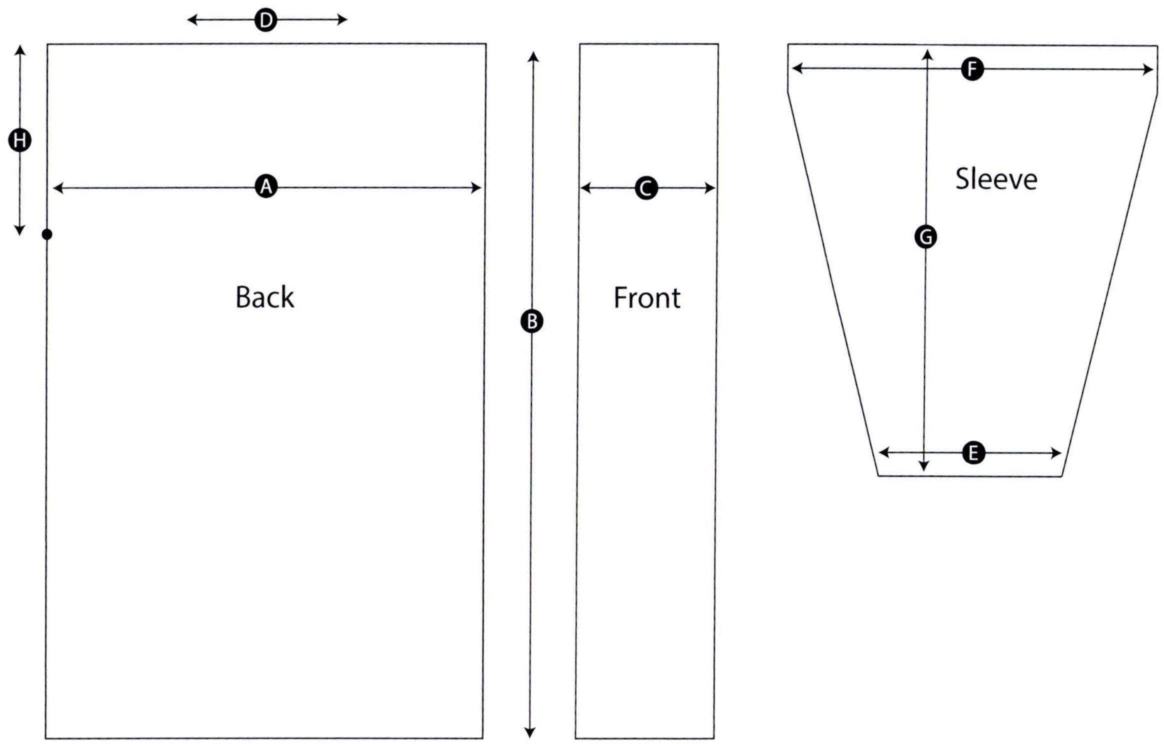

Place a marker on each side of Front and Back {8-8-8½}{8½-9-9}"/ {20.5-20.5-21.5}{21.5-23-23} cm down from shoulder seam.

Sew sleeves to Body between markers.

Weave underarm and side in one continuous seam *(Fig. 16, page 95)*.

Schematic Label	Description	Imperial Measurement / Metric Measurement
A	Width across Back	{19-21½-23¾}{26¼-28½-31}" / {48.5-54.5-60.5}{66.5-72.5-78.5} cm
B	Total Length	29" / 73.5 cm
C	Width across Front	{5¾-7-8¼}{9½-10½-11¾}" / {14.5-18-21}{24-26.5-30} cm
D	Neck Width	7" / 18 cm
E	Sleeve Width at Cuff	8½" / 21.5 cm
F	Sleeve Width at Upper Arm	{16-16-17¼}{17¼-18-18}" / {40.5-40.5-44}{44-45.5-45.5} cm
G	Sleeve Length	{19-18¼-17}{15¾-15-14}" / {48.5-46.5-43}{40-38-35.5} cm
H	Armhole Depth	{8-8-8.5}{8.5-9-9}" / {20.5-20.5-21.5}{21.5-23-23} cm

Hoodie

●●○○ EASY

SHOPPING LIST

Yarn (Bulky Weight) BULKY 5

[5 ounces, 132 yards
(141 grams, 121 meters) per skein]:

☐ {6-7-7}{8-8-9} skeins

Knitting Needles

29" (73.5 cm) Circular,

☐ Size 10½ (6.5 mm)
or size needed for gauge

16" (40.5 cm) Circular,

☐ Size 10½ (6.5 mm)

Double-pointed -2,

☐ Size 10½ (6.5 mm)

Additional Supplies

☐ Stitch markers - 2

☐ Yarn needle

SIZE INFORMATION

Finished Chest Measurement:
{36¼-40-43¾}{48½-52¼-56)"/
{92-101.5-111}{123-133-142} cm

Finished Length:
{26-26-26½}{26½-27-27}"/
{66-66-67.5}{67.5-68.5-68.5} cm

Size Note: For ease in following the pattern, we have printed the instructions for each size in a different color:

- Size Small in Blue
- Size Medium in Pink
- Size Large in Green
- Size 1X in Red
- Size 2X in Purple
- Size 3X in Orange

GAUGE INFORMATION

In Stockinette Stitch,
13 sts and 19 rows = 4" (10 cm)

TECHNIQUES USED

- YO ***(Photo G, page 7)***
- K2 tog ***(Photo K, page 7)***
- SSK ***(Photos L & M, page 8)***
- S2KP2 ***(Photos N thru P, page 8)***
- M1 ***(Figs. 5a & b, page 93)***
- P2 tog ***(Fig. 10, page 94)***
- SSP ***(Fig. 12, page 94)***

FRONT

Ribbing

Cast on {60-66-72}{80-86-92} sts.

Work in K1, P1 ribbing for 2" (5 cm), increasing one st on last row: {61-67-73}{81-87-93} sts.

Body

Beginning with a **knit** row, work in Stockinette Stitch until piece measures approximately 16½" (42 cm) from cast on edge, ending by working a **purl** row.

ARMHOLE SHAPING

Note: Maintain established pattern throughout.

Rows 1 and 2: Bind off {4-4-6}{6-8-8} sts, work across: {53-59-61}{69-71-77} sts.

Work even until Front measures approximately {22-22-22½}{22½-23-23}"/{56-56-57}{57-58.5-58.5} cm from cast on edge, ending by working a **purl** row.

NECK SHAPING

Note: Both sides of Neck are worked at the same time, using separate yarn for each side.

Row 1: Knit {20-23-24}{28-29-32} sts; with second ball, bind off next 13 sts, knit across: {20-23-24}{28-29-32} sts **each** side.

Rows 2-5: Work across; with second yarn, bind off 2 sts, work across: {16-19-20}{24-25-28} sts **each** side.

Row 6: Work across to within 2 sts of Neck edge, SSP; with second yarn, P2 tog, purl across: {15-18-19} {23-24-27} sts **each** side.

Work even until Front measures approximately {25-25-25½} {25½-26-26}"/ {63.5-63.5-65}{65-66-66} cm from cast on edge, ending by working a **purl** row.

SHOULDER SHAPING

Rows 1 and 2: Bind off {8-9-10} {12-12-14} sts, work across; with second yarn, work across: {7-9-9} {11-12-13} sts **each** side.

Row 3: Bind off sts to Neck edge; with second yarn, knit across.

Row 4: Bind off remaining sts.

BACK

Work same as Front until Back measures approximately {9¼-9¼-9¾} {9¾-10¼-10¼}"/{23.5-23.5-25} {25-26-26} cm from cast on edge, ending by working a **purl** row : {61-67-73}{81-87-93} sts.

Lace Motif

Note: Begin working Lace Motif over center **35 sts** and **AT THE SAME TIME**, when Back measures same as Front to Armhole Shaping, work Armhole Shaping same as Front.

Row 1: Knit {13-16-19}{23-26-29} sts, place marker, K4, YO, SSK, K 23, K2 tog, YO, K4, place marker, knit across.

Row 2 AND ALL WRONG SIDE ROWS: Purl across slipping markers.

Row 3: Knit to marker, slip marker, (K5, YO, SSK) twice, K7, (K2 tog, YO, K5) twice, slip marker, knit across.

Row 5: Knit to marker, slip marker, K6, YO, SSK, K2, K2 tog, YO, K1, YO, SSK, K5, K2 tog, YO, K1, YO, SSK, K2, K2 tog, YO, K6, slip marker, knit across.

Row 7: Knit to marker, slip marker, K7, YO, SSK, K1, K2 tog, YO, K2, YO, SSK, K3, K2 tog, YO, K2, YO, SSK, K1, K2 tog, YO, K7, slip marker, knit across.

Row 9: Knit to marker, slip marker, K8, YO, SSK, K2 tog, YO, K3, YO, SSK, K1, K2 tog, YO K3, YO, SSK, K2 tog, YO, K8, slip marker, knit across.

Row 11: Knit to marker, slip marker, K 10, K2 tog, YO, K4, YO, S2KP2, YO, K4, YO, SSK, K 10, slip marker, knit across.

Row 13: Repeat Row 11.

Row 15: Knit to marker, slip marker, K8, K2 tog, YO, K2, YO, SSK, K2, YO, S2KP2, YO, K2, K2 tog, YO, K2, YO, SSK, K8, slip marker, knit across.

Row 17: Knit to marker, slip marker, K7, K2 tog, YO, K1, (YO, SSK, K1) twice, YO, S2KP2, YO, K1, (K2 tog, YO, K1) twice, YO, SSK, K7, slip marker, knit across.

Row 19: Knit to marker, slip marker, K6, K2 tog, YO, K3, YO, SSK, K1, YO, SSK, YO, S2KP2, YO, K2 tog, YO, K1, K2 tog, YO, K3, YO, SSK, K6, slip marker, knit across.

Row 21: Knit to marker, slip marker, K1, K2 tog, YO, K2, K2 tog, YO, K5, (YO, SSK, K1) twice, K2 tog, YO, K1, K2 tog, YO, K5, YO, SSK, K2, YO, SSK, K1, slip marker, knit across.

Row 23: Knit to marker, slip marker, K1, YO, S2KP2, YO, K2 tog, YO, K7, YO, SSK, K5, K2 tog, YO, K7, YO, SSK, YO, S2KP2, YO, K1, slip marker, knit across.

Row 25: Knit to marker, slip marker, YO, SSK, K1, K2 tog, YO, K9, K2 tog, YO, K3, YO, SSK, K9, YO, SSK, K1, K2 tog, YO, slip marker, knit across.

Row 27: Knit to marker, slip marker, K1, YO, S2KP2, YO, K1, YO, SSK, K3, (K2 tog, YO, K1) twice, YO, S2KP2, YO, (K1, YO, SSK) twice, K3, K2 tog, YO, K1, YO, S2KP2, YO, K1, slip marker, knit across.

Row 29: Knit to marker, slip marker, K1, K2 tog, YO, K3, YO, SSK, (K1, K2 tog, YO) twice, K2, YO, S2KP2, YO, K2, (YO, SSK, K1) twice, K2 tog, YO, K3, YO, SSK, K1, slip marker, knit across.

Row 31: Knit to marker, slip marker, K7, YO, S2KP2, YO, K1, K2 tog, YO, K3, YO, S2KP2, YO, K3, YO, SSK, K1, YO, S2KP2, YO, K7, slip marker, knit across.

Row 33: Knit to marker, slip marker, K7, K2 tog, YO, K1, K2 tog, YO, K4, YO, S2KP2, YO, K4, YO, SSK, K1, YO, SSK, K7, slip marker, knit across.

KEY

knit on RS; purl on WS

K2 tog

SSK

YO

S2KP2

Work Rows 1-48 for pattern.

Follow chart from right to left on RS rows; follow chart from left to right on WS rows.

LACE MOTIF

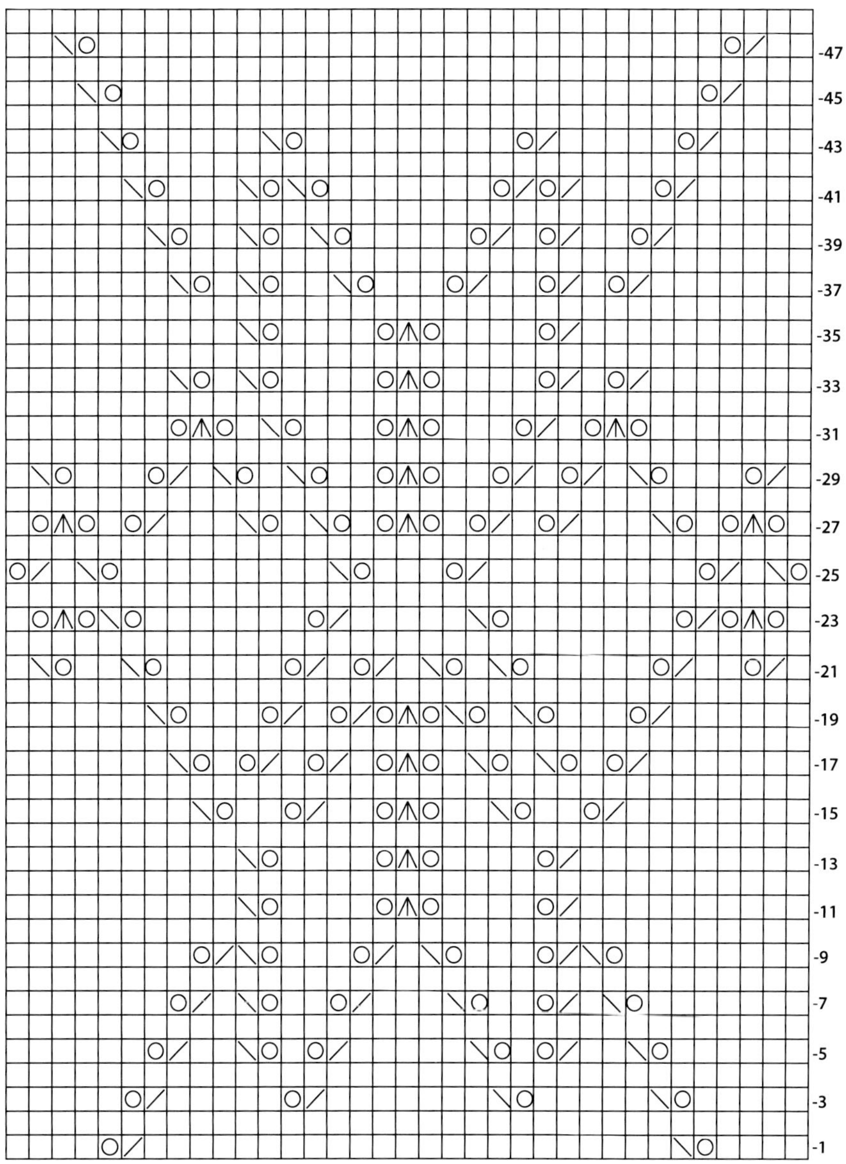

Row 35: Knit to marker, slip marker, K 10, K2 tog, YO, K4, YO, S2KP2, YO, K4, YO, SSK, K 10, slip marker, knit across.

Row 37: Knit to marker, slip marker, K7, K2 tog, YO, K1, K2 tog, YO, K2, K2 tog, YO, K3, YO, SSK, K2, YO, SSK, K1, YO, SSK, K7, slip marker, knit across.

Row 39: Knit to marker, slip marker, K6, K2 tog, YO, K2, K2 tog, YO, K1, K2 tog, YO, K5, YO, SSK, K1, YO, SSK, K2, YO, SSK, K6, slip marker, knit across.

Row 41: Knit to marker, slip marker, K5, K2 tog, YO, K3, (K2 tog, YO) twice, K7, (YO, SSK) twice, K3, YO, SSK, K5, slip marker, knit across.

Row 43: Knit to marker, slip marker, K4, K2 tog, YO, K5, K2 tog, YO, K9, YO, SSK, K5, YO, SSK, K4, slip marker, knit across.

Row 45: Knit to marker, slip marker, K3, K2 tog, YO, K 25, YO, SSK, K3, slip marker, knit across.

Row 47: Knit to marker, slip marker, K2, K2 tog, YO, K 27, YO, SSK, K2, slip marker, knit across.

Work in Stockinette Stitch until Back measures approximately {25-25-25½}{25½-26-26}"/{63.5-63.5-65}{65-66-66} cm from cast on edge, ending by working a **purl** row: {53-59-61}{69-71-77} sts.

SHOULDER SHAPING

Rows 1 and 2: Bind off {8-9-10}{12-12-14} sts, work across: {37-41-41}{45-47-49} sts.

Rows 3 and 4: Bind off {7-9-9}{11-12-13} sts, work across: 23 sts.

Bind off remaining sts in **knit**.

SLEEVE (Make 2)

Ribbing

Cast on 30 sts.

Work in K1, P1 ribbing for 2" (5 cm).

Body

Beginning with a **knit** row, work in Stockinette Stitch, increasing one st at each edge, every {6-4-4}{4-2-2} rows, {13-1-10}{12-4-5} time(s); then increase every {0-6-6}{6-4-4} rows, {0-12-5}{3-13-12} times ***(see Zeros, page 91)***: {56-56-60}{60-64-64} sts.

Work even until Sleeve measures approximately {20½-20-19½}{18½-18-17½}" / {52-51-49.5}{47-45.5-44.5} cm from cast on edge, ending by working a **purl** row.

Bind off all sts in **knit**.

FINISHING

Sew shoulder seams.

Hood

With **right** side facing, using 16" (40.5 cm) circular needle, and beginning at center front neck, pick up 71 sts evenly spaced around neck edge ***(Figs. 13a & b, page 94)***; do **not** join.

Row 1: (P1, K1) 3 times, purl across to last 6 sts, (K1, P1) 3 times.

Row 2 (RS)**:** (K1, P1) 3 times, knit across to last 6 sts, (P1, K1) 3 times.

Repeat Rows 1 and 2 until Hood measures approximately 1" (2.5 cm), ending by working a **wrong** side row.

Next Row (Increase row)**:** (K1, P1) 3 times, K 29, M1, place marker, K1, place marker, M1, knit across to last 6 sts, (P1, K1) 3 times: 73 sts.

Maintaining pattern, continue to increase one st on each side of center stitch, every 6 rows, 5 times **more**: 83 sts.

Work even until Hood measures approximately 12½" (32 cm) from cast on edge, ending by working a **wrong** side row and decreasing one st at center of last row: 82 sts.

Divide the stitches evenly on two double-pointed needles.

Holding stitches with **right** sides together, work three needle bind off *(Fig. 15, page 95)*.

Front Pocket (Optional)

Cast on 59 sts.

Row 1: (P1, K1) 3 times, purl across to last 6 sts, (K1, P1) 3 times.

Row 2 (RS)**:** (K1, P1) 3 times, knit across to last 6 sts, (P1, K1) 3 times.

Row 3: (P1, K1) 3 times, purl across to last 6 sts, (K1, P1) 3 times.

Row 4 (Decrease row)**:** (K1, P1) 3 times, SSK, knit across to last 8 sts, K2 tog, (P1, K1) 3 times: 57 sts.

Maintaining pattern, continue to decrease one st at each edge, every other rows, 5 times **more**; then decrease every 4 rows, 6 times: 35 sts.

Bind off all sts in pattern.

Using photo as a guide, sew the lower and upper edges of pocket to Front, leaving sides open.

Set in sleeves.

Weave underarm and side in one continuous seam *(Fig. 16, page 95)*.

Schematic Label	Description	Imperial Measurement / Metric Measurement
A	Front and Back Width	{18¼-20-21¾}{24¼-26¼-28}" / {46.5-51-55}{61.5-66.5-71} cm
B	Body Length to Underarm	16½" / 42 cm
C	Body Length to Neck Shaping	{22-22-22½}{22½-23-23}" / {56-56-57}{57-58.5-58.5} cm
D	Body Length to Shoulder Shaping	{25-25-25½}{25½-26-26}" / {63.5-63.5-65}{65-66-66} cm
E	Neck Width	7" / 18 cm
F	Front Neck Depth	3" / 7.5 cm
G	Shoulder Shaping	1" / 2.5 cm
H	Sleeve Width at Cuff	9" / 23 cm
I	Sleeve Length	{20½-20-19½}{18½-18-17½}" / {52-51-49.5}{47-45.5-44.5} cm
J	Sleeve Width at Upper Arm	{17¼-17¼-18½}{18½-19¾-19¾}" / {44-44-47}{47-50-50} cm

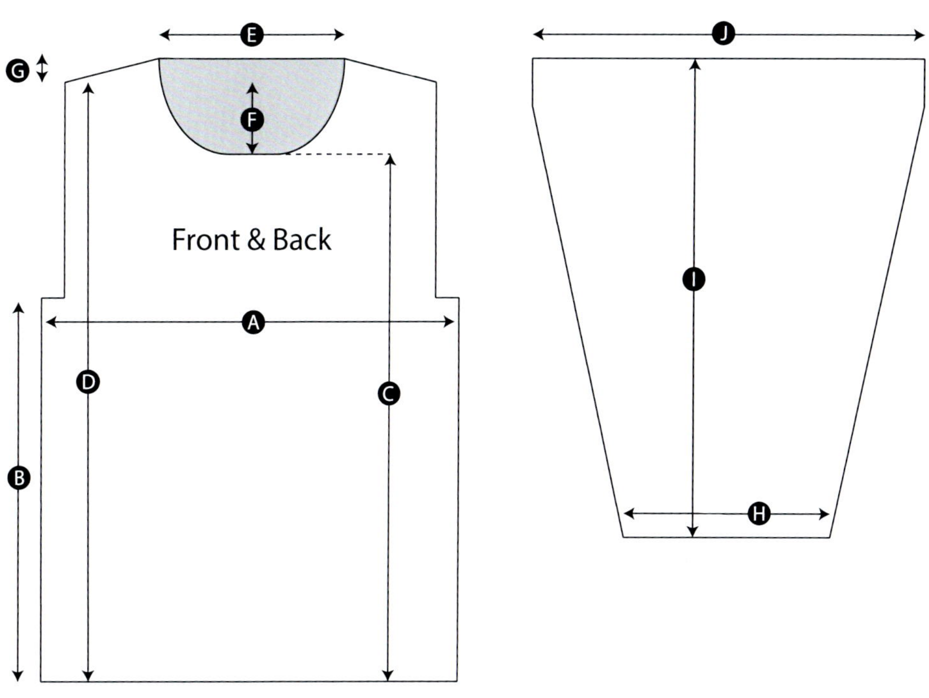

Mandala Shawl

●●○○ **EASY**

Finished Size:

Approximately 54" wide x 22"deep (137 cm x 56 cm), blocked

SHOPPING LIST

Yarn (Light Weight) LIGHT 3

[5.3 ounces, 590 yards (150 grams, 540 meters) per ball]:

☐ One ball

Knitting Needles

29" (73.5 cm) Circular,

☐ Size 9 (5.5 mm)

or size needed for gauge

Additional Supplies

☐ Crochet hook size H (5 mm) (for provisional cast on)

☐ Scrap yarn

☐ Yarn needle

GAUGE INFORMATION

In First Lace Section pattern, 16 sts and 22 rows = 4" (10 cm), blocked.

TECHNIQUES USED

- YO *(Photos G & H, page 7)*
- K2 tog *(Photo K, page 7)*
- SSK *(Photos L & M, page 8)*
- SSSK *(see Decreases, page 8)*
- S2KP2 *(Photos N thru P, page 8)*
- M1 *(Figs. 5a & b, page 93)*
- K2 tog tbl *(Fig. 9, page 94)*

SHAWL

Garter Tab & First Section

With the scrap yarn, work provisional cast on as follows: With crochet hook, ch 7. Cut the yarn and pull the end through the last chain made to secure it. Tie a loose knot on this tail to mark it as the end you'll use later to unravel the chain.

Working in back ridge of crocheted chain *(Fig. 14, page 95)* and using knitting needle, pick up one st in each of center 3 chs: 3 sts.

Row 1-6: Beginning with a **purl** row, work 6 rows in Stockinette Stitch.

Rotate piece 90°; pick up 3 sts across side edge *(Figs. 13a & b, page 94)*; rotate piece 90° again; unzip provisional cast on, with needle at opposite end, pick up 3 live stitches across provisional cast on edge and knit them: 9 sts.

Row 7: Purl across slipping markers.

Row 8 (Right side)**:** K3, place marker, YO, K1, YO, place marker, K1, place marker, YO, K1, YO, place marker, K3: 13 sts.

Row 9 AND ALL WRONG SIDE ROWS TO FIRST LACE SECTION: Purl across slipping markers.

Row 10: K3, slip marker, YO, knit to marker, YO, slip marker, K1, slip marker, YO, knit to marker, YO, slip marker, K3: 17 sts.

Row 12: K3, slip marker, YO, purl to marker, YO, slip marker, K1, slip marker, YO, purl to marker, YO, slip marker, K3: 21 sts.

Row 14: K3, slip marker, YO, knit to marker, YO, slip marker, K1, slip marker, YO, knit to marker, YO, slip marker, K3: 25 sts.

Row 16: K3, slip marker, YO, knit to marker, YO, slip marker, K1, slip marker, YO, knit to marker, YO, slip marker, K3: 29 sts.

Rows 17-100: Repeat Rows 12-17, 14 times: 197 sts.

First Lace Section

Row 1: K3, slip marker, YO, K1, M1, knit to within one st of marker, M1, K1, YO, slip marker, K1, slip marker, YO, K1, M1, knit to within one st of marker, M1, K1, YO, slip marker, K3: 205 sts.

Row 2: P3, slip marker, knit to marker, slip marker, P1, slip marker, knit to marker, slip marker, P3.

Row 3: K3, slip marker, YO, knit to marker, YO, slip marker, K1, slip marker, YO, knit to marker, YO, slip marker, K3: 209 sts.

Rows 4 and 5: Repeat Rows 2 and 3: 213 sts.

Row 6: Purl across slipping markers.

Row 7: K3, † slip marker, YO, K1, ★ K2 tog, YO, K1, YO, SSK; repeat from ★ to within one st of marker, K1, YO, slip marker †, K1, repeat from † to † once, K3: 217 sts.

Row 8: Purl across slipping markers.

Row 9: K3, † slip marker, YO, ★ K1, K2 tog, YO, K3, YO, SSK; repeat from ★ to within one st of marker, K1, YO, slip marker †, K1, repeat from † to † once, K3: 221 sts.

Row 10: Purl across slipping markers.

Row 11: K3, † slip marker, YO, K1, K2 tog, YO, K5, ★ YO, SSSK, YO, K5; repeat from ★ to within 3 sts of marker, YO, SSK, K1, YO, slip marker †, K1, repeat from † to † once, K3: 225 sts.

FIRST LACE SECTION

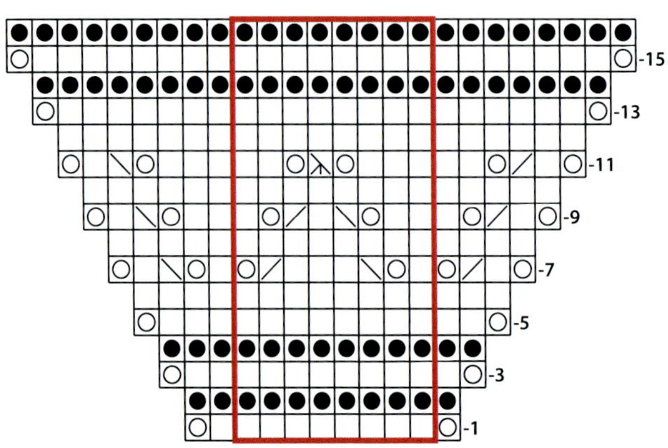

KEY

- knit on RS; purl on WS
- knit on WS
- YO
- K2 tog
- SSK
- SSSK
- pattern repeat

Work Rows 1-16.

Follow chart from right to left on RS rows; follow chart from left to right on WS rows.

Row 12: Purl across slipping markers.

Row 13: K3, slip marker, YO, knit to marker, YO, slip marker, K1, slip marker, YO, knit to marker, YO, slip marker, K3: 229 sts.

Row 14: P3, slip marker, knit to marker, slip marker, P1, slip marker, knit to marker, slip marker, K3.

Rows 15 and 16: Repeat Rows 13 and 14: 233 sts.

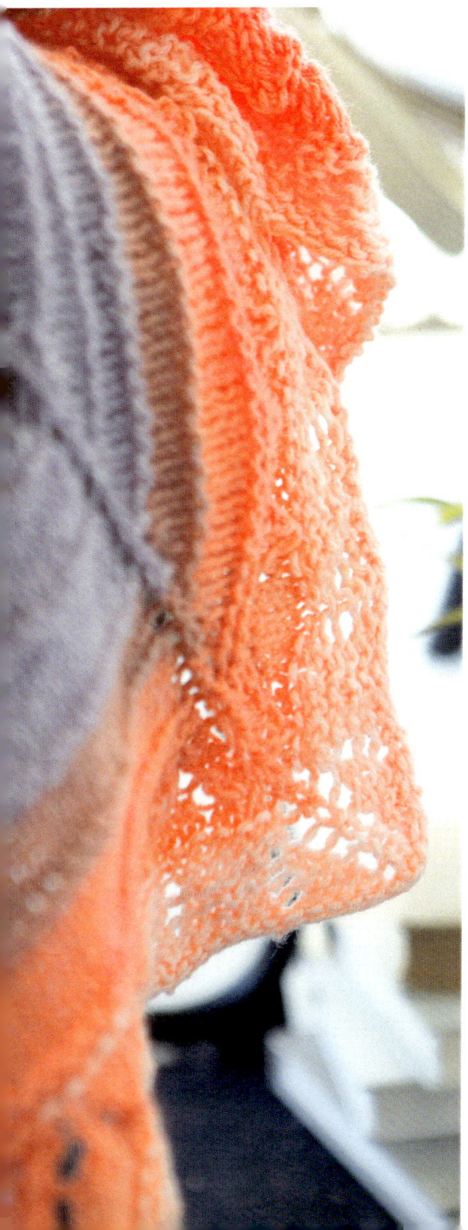

Second Lace Section

Row 1: K3, † slip marker, YO, K1, ★ YO, SSK, K3, K2 tog, YO, K1; repeat from ★ to marker, YO, slip marker †, K1, repeat from † to † once, K3: 237 sts.

Row 2 AND ALL WRONG SIDE ROWS: P3, slip marker, knit to marker, slip marker, P1, slip marker, knit to marker, slip marker, P3.

Row 3: K3, † slip marker, YO, K2, ★ YO, K1, SSK, K1, K2 tog, K1, YO, K1; repeat from ★ to within one st of marker, K1, YO, slip marker †, K1, repeat from † to † once, K3: 241 sts.

Row 5: K3, † slip marker, YO, K3, YO, K2, S2KP2, K2, ★ YO, K1, YO, K2, S2KP2, K2; repeat from ★ to within 3 sts of marker, YO, K3, YO, slip marker †, K1, repeat from † to † once, K3: 245 sts.

Row 7: K3, † slip marker, YO, K4, YO, K2, S2KP2, K2, ★ YO, K1, YO, K2, S2KP2, K2; repeat from ★ to within 4 sts of marker, YO, K4, YO, slip marker †, K1, repeat from † to † once, K3: 245 sts.

Row 8: P3, slip marker, knit to marker, slip marker, P1, slip marker, knit to marker, slip marker, P3.

Finishing

Bind off using stretchy lace bind off as follows ***(see Super Stretchy Bind Off, page 6)***:

K2, ★ return the 2 sts back to the left needle, K2 tog tbl, K1; repeat from ★ across until all sts have been bound off.

SECOND LACE SECTION

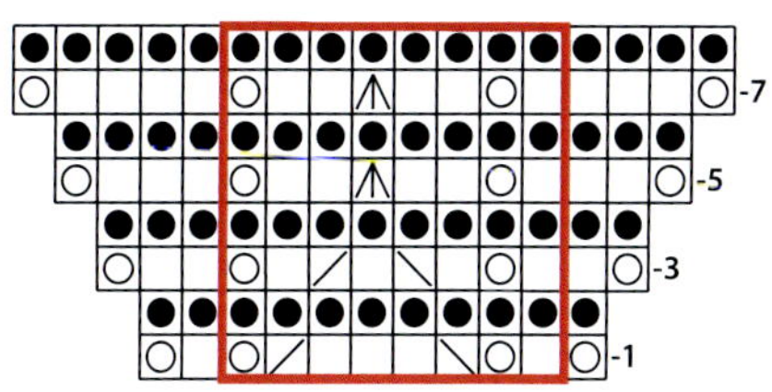

KEY

- knit on RS; purl on WS
- knit on WS
- YO
- K2 tog
- SSK
- S2KP2
- pattern repeat

Work Rows 1-8.

Follow chart from right to left on RS rows; follow chart from left to right on WS rows.

Boho Vest

●●○○ EASY

SHOPPING LIST

Yarn (Medium Weight) MEDIUM 4

[16 ounces, 867 yards

(454 grams, 792 meters) per skein]:

☐ {1-1-1}{1-2-2} skein(s)

Knitting Needles

29" (73.5 cm) Circular,

☐ Size 8 (5 mm)

or size needed for gauge

Double-pointed needles,

☐ Size 8 (5 mm)

Additional Supplies

☐ Stitch markers - 8

☐ Split ring marker

☐ Scrap yarn for st holders

☐ Yarn needle

SIZE INFORMATION

Finished Chest Measurement:

{36-37-41}{43-44-48}"/

{91.5-94-104}{109-112-122} cm

Finished Length:

{21½-22-22½}{23-23½-24}"/

{54.5-56-57}{58.5-59.5-61} cm

Size Note: For ease in following the pattern, we have printed the instructions for each size in a different color:

- Size Small in Blue
- Size Medium in Pink
- Size Large in Green
- Size 1X in Red
- Size 2X in Purple
- Size 3X in Orange

GAUGE INFORMATION

In Stockinette Stitch,

16 sts and 19 rows = 4" (10 cm)

TECHNIQUES USED

- YO *(Photos G & J, page 7)*
- K2 tog *(Photo K, page 7)*
- SSK *(Photos L & M, page 8*
- Knit Increase *(Figs. 3a & b, page 92)*
- P2 tog *(Fig. 10, page 94)*

VEST

Body

Beginning at neck edge, cast on {96-96-96}{100-100-100} sts.

Rows 1-3: Knit across.

Row 4: K2, bind off next 3 sts (buttonhole), knit across.

Row 5 (RS)**:** Knit across to bound off sts, **turn**; add on 3 sts ***(Figs. 8a & b, page 93)***, **turn**; K2.

Rows 6 and 7: Knit across.

Row 8: Knit across increasing {10-12-14}{14-16-18} sts evenly spaced ***(see Increasing Evenly Across A Row, page 92)***: {106-108-110} {114-116-118} sts.

Row 9: Knit {18-19-20}{21-21-23} sts, place marker, K1, place marker, knit {16-16-14}{14-14-12} sts, place marker, K1, place marker, knit {34-34-38}{40-42-44} sts, place marker, K1, place marker, knit {16-16-14}{14-14-12} sts, place marker, K1, place marker, knit {18-19-20}{21-21-23} sts.

Row 10: K4, purl across to last 4 sts, slipping markers, K4.

Row 11 (Increase row)**:** ★ Knit to marker, YO, slip marker, K1, slip marker, YO; repeat from ★ 3 times **more**, knit across: {114-116-118} {122-124-126} sts.

Rows 12 thru {37-39-43}{45-47-51}: Repeat Rows 10 and 11, {13-14-16} {17-18-20} times: {218-228-246} {258-268-286} sts.

Row {38-40-44}{46-48-52}: Removing all markers, K4, purl across to last 4 sts, K4.

SEPARATE BODY & SLEEVES

Row 1: Knit {33-35-38}{40-41-45} sts, slip next {44-46-48}{50-52-54} sts to holder for sleeve, **turn**; add on 8 sts, **turn**; knit {64-66-74}{78-82-88} sts for back, slip next {44-46-48}{50-52-54} sts to holder for second sleeve, **turn**; add on 8 sts, **turn**; knit across: {146-152-166}{174-180-194} sts.

Row 2: Knit across increasing {2-0-2}{2-0-2) sts evenly spaced ***(see Zeros, page 91)***: {148-152-168}{176-180-196} sts.

Rows 3 and 4: Knit across.

Row 5: K4, place marker, ★ K2, YO, SSK; repeat from ★ across to last 4 sts, place marker, K4.

Row 6: K4, slip marker, ★ P2, YO, P2 tog; repeat from ★ across to marker, slip marker, K4.

Row 7: K4, slip marker, ★ K2, YO, SSK; repeat from ★ across to marker, slip marker, K4.

Repeat Rows 6 and 7 until Vest measures approximately {20½-21-21½}{22-22½-23}"/{52-53.5-54.5}{56-57-58.5} cm from cast on edge, ending by working a **wrong** side row.

BOTTOM BAND

Row 1: Knit across decreasing {15-16-17}{18-19-20} sts evenly spaced: {133-136-149}{158-161-176} sts.

Work in Garter St for 1" (2.5 cm), ending by working a **wrong** side row.

Bind off all sts.

Finishing

SLEEVE EDGING

With the **right** side facing and using a double-pointed needle, pick up 8 sts along underarm ***(Figs. 13a & b, page 94)***, slip {44-46-48}{50-52-54} sts from sleeve holder onto double-pointed needles, dividing all sts evenly among double-pointed needles, knit across; place split ring marker around first st to mark beginning of round ***(see Circular Knitting, page 92)***: {52-54-56}{58-60-62} sts.

Rnd 1: Purl around.

Rnd 2: Knit around.

Rnd 3: Purl around.

Bind off all sts in **knit**.

Repeat for second sleeve edging.

KNIT BUTTON (Optional)

Cast on one st.

Row 1: Knit increase: 2 sts.

Row 2: Knit increase twice: 4 sts.

Rows 3-6: Knit increase, knit across to last st, knit increase: 12 sts.

Rows 7-12: Knit across.

Rows 13-16: SSK, knit across to last 2 sts, K2 tog: 4 sts.

Row 17: SSK, K2 tog: 2 sts.

Row 18: K2 tog; cut yarn leaving a long end for sewing.

Thread yarn needle with long end and weave needle around the outer edge of button. Pull to gather, stuffing with yarn ends before closing. Use same end to attach button to Neckband opposite buttonhole.

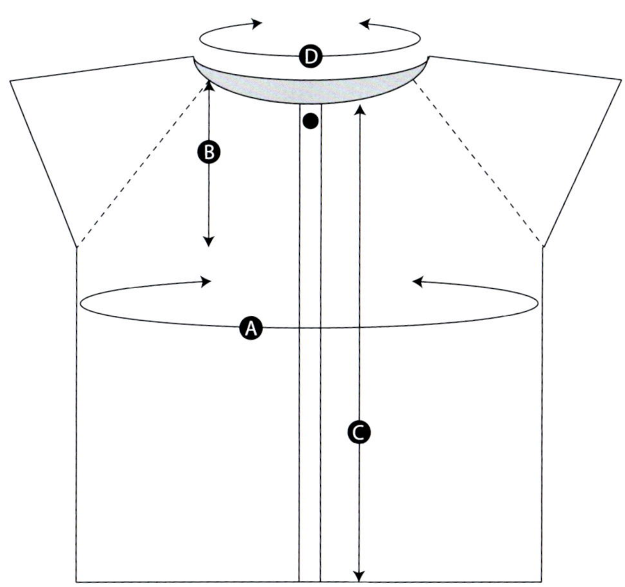

Schematic Label	Description	Imperial Measurement / Metric Measurement
A	Chest Measurement	{36-37-41}{43-44-48}" / {91.5-94-104}{109-112-122} cm
B	Armhole Depth	{7¾-8¼-9}{9½-10-10¾}" / {19.5-21-23}{24-25.5-27.5} cm
C	Total Length	{21½-22-22½}{23-23½-24}" / {54.5-56-57}{58.5-59.5-61} cm
D	Neck Circumference	{23-23-23}{24-24-24}" / {58.5-58.5-58.5}{61-61-61} cm

Baby Blanket

●●○○ **EASY**

Finished Measurement:
34" x 34" (86.5 cm x 86..5 cm), blocked

SHOPPING LIST

Yarn (Medium Weight) MEDIUM 4
[7 ounces, 370 yards
(198 grams, 338 meters) per skein]:
☐ 2 skeins

Knitting Needles
29" (73.5 cm) Circular,
☐ Size 10½ (6.5 mm)
or size needed for gauge
Double-pointed (set of 5),
☐ Size 10½ (6.5 mm)

Additional Supplies
☐ Crochet hook, size I (5.5 mm)
☐ Yarn needle

GAUGE INFORMATION

In pattern,
13 sts and 22½ rnds = 4" (10 cm), blocked.

TECHNIQUES USED

- YO *(Photo G, page 7)*
- K2 tog *(Photo K, page 7)*
- SSK *(Photos L & M, page 8)*
- S2KP2 *(Photos N thru P, page 8)*

Blanket

Step 1: Leaving a 6" (15 cm) tail, make a loop in the yarn *(see Beginning Ring, page 6)*.

Step 2: Insert crochet hook in center of loop, YO and pull working yarn through.

Step 3: YO and draw through loop on hook (one loop on hook).

Step 4: Insert crochet hook in center of loop, YO and pull working yarn through.

Step 5: YO and draw through last loop on hook (2 loops on hook).

Step 6: Repeat Steps 4 and 5, 6 times more (8 loops on hook).

Step 7: Distribute 2 loops to each of 4 double-pointed needles. Tug on the yarn tail to tighten the loop.

Set Up Round (Right side)**:** Knit around: 8 sts.

First Lace Section

Rnd 1 (Right side)**:** ★ YO, K1, YO, place marker, K1, place marker; repeat from ★ around, making last st marker a contrasting color indicating beginning of round: 16 sts.

Rnd 2 AND ALL WRONG SIDE RNDS THRU RND 68: Knit around, slipping markers.

Rnd 3: ★ YO, K3, YO, slip marker, K1, slip marker; repeat from ★ around: 24 sts.

Rnd 5: ★ YO, K2 tog, YO, K1, YO, SSK, YO, slip marker, K1, slip marker; repeat from ★ around: 32 sts.

Rnd 7: ★ YO, K1, (YO, SSK, K1, K2 tog, YO, K1) to marker, YO, slip marker, K1, slip marker; repeat from ★ around: 40 sts.

Rnd 9: ★ YO, K2, YO, SSK, K1, K2 tog, (YO, K1, YO, SSK, K1, K2 tog) to within 2 sts of marker, YO, K2, YO, slip marker, K1, slip marker; repeat from ★ around: 48 sts.

Rnd 11: ★ YO, K2 tog, YO, K1, YO, SSK, (K1, K2 tog, YO, K1, YO, SSK) to marker, YO, slip marker, K1, slip marker; repeat from ★ around: 56 sts.

Rnd 13: ★ YO, K1, YO, SSK, K1, K2 tog, YO, K1, (YO, SSK, K1, K2 tog, YO, K1) to marker, YO, slip marker, K1, slip marker; repeat from ★ around: 64 sts.

Rnd 15: ★ YO, K2, YO, SSK, K1, K2 tog, (YO, K1, YO, SSK, K1, K2 tog) to within 2 sts of marker, YO, K2, YO, slip marker, K1, slip marker; repeat from ★ around: 72 sts.

Rnd 17: ★ YO, K3, YO, SSK, K1, K2 tog, (YO, K1, YO, SSK, K1, K2 tog) to within 3 sts of marker, YO, K3, YO, slip marker, K1, slip marker; repeat from ★ around: 80 sts.

Rnds 19-66: Repeat Rnds 7-18, 4 times: 272 sts.

First Eyelet Ridge

Rnd 1: ★ YO, knit to marker, YO, slip marker, K1, slip marker; repeat from ★ around: 280 sts.

Rnd 2: Purl around, slipping markers.

Rnd 3: ★ (YO, K2 tog) to within one st of marker, K1, YO, slip marker, K1, slip marker; repeat from ★ around: 288 sts.

Rnd 4: Purl around, slipping markers.

Center Section

Rnd 1: ★ YO, knit to marker, YO, slip marker, K1, slip marker; repeat from ★ around: 296 sts.

Rnd 2: Knit around, slipping markers.

Rnds 3-16: Repeat Rnds 1 and 2, 7 times: 352 sts.

Second Eyelet Ridge

Rnd 1: ★ YO, knit to marker, YO, slip marker, K1, slip marker; repeat from ★ around: 360 sts.

Rnd 2: Purl around, slipping markers.

Rnd 3: ★ (YO, K2 tog) to within one st of marker, K1, YO, slip marker, K1, slip marker; repeat from ★ around: 368 sts.

Rnd 4: Purl around, slipping markers.

Border Lace

Rnd 1: ★ (YO, K1) twice, S2KP2, [K1, (YO, K1) twice, S2KP2] to within 2 sts of marker, (K1, YO) twice, slip marker, K1, slip marker; repeat from ★ around: 376 sts.

Rnd 2 AND ALL EVEN NUMBERED RNDS THRU RND 10: Knit around.

FIRST LACE SECTION

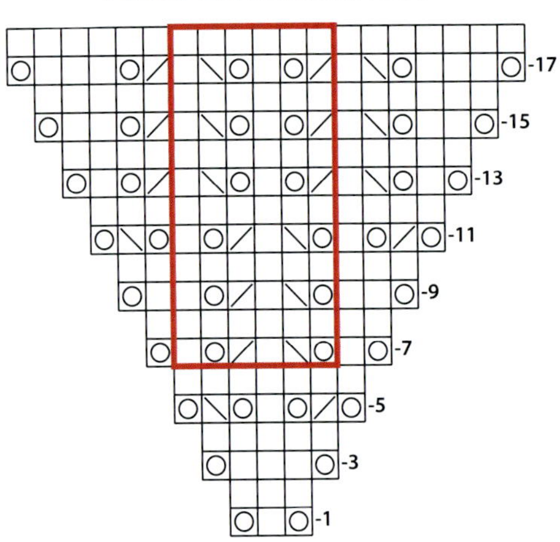

KEY
- knit
- YO
- K2 tog
- SSK
- pattern repeat

Work Rnds 1-18; then repeat Rnds 7-18.
Follow chart from right to left on all rnds.

EYELET RIDGE

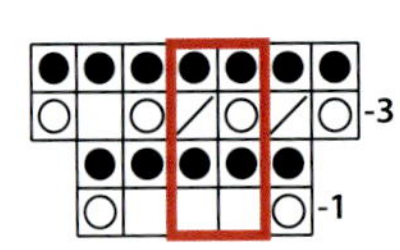

KEY
- knit
- purl
- YO
- K2 tog
- pattern repeat

Work Rnds 1-4.
Follow chart from right to left on all rnds.

Rnd 3: ★ YO, K2, YO, K1, S2KP2, K1, [(YO, K1) twice, S2KP2, K1] to within 2 sts of marker, YO, K2, YO, slip marker, K1, slip marker; repeat from ★ around: 384 sts.

Rnd 5: ★ YO, K3, YO, K1, S2KP2, K1, [(YO, K1) twice, S2KP2, K1] to within 3 sts of marker, YO, K3, YO, slip marker, K1, slip marker; repeat from ★ around: 392 sts.

Rnd 7: ★ YO, K2 tog, K1, (YO, K1) twice, [S2KP2, K1, (YO, K1) twice] to within 2 sts of marker, SSK, YO, slip marker, K1, slip marker; repeat from ★ around: 400 sts.

Rnd 9: ★ YO, K1, K2 tog, K1, (YO, K1) twice, [S2KP2, K1, (YO, K1) twice] to within 3 sts of marker, SSK, K1, YO, slip marker, K1, slip marker; repeat from ★ around: 408 sts.

Rnd 11: ★ YO, K2, K2 tog, K1, (YO, K1) twice, [S2KP2, K1, (YO, K1) twice] to within 4 sts of marker, SSK, K2, YO, slip marker, K1, slip marker; repeat from ★ around: 416 sts.

Rnd 12: Knit around.

Bind off all sts loosely in **knit**.

BORDER LACE

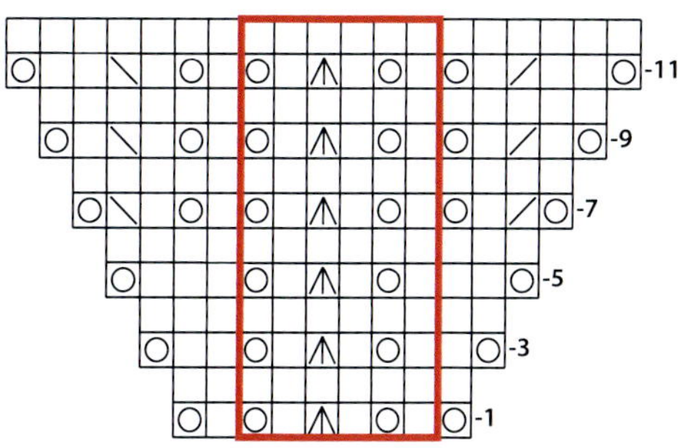

KEY
- knit on RS; purl on WS
- YO
- K2 tog
- SSK
- S2KP2
- pattern repeat

Work Rnds 1-12.

Follow chart from right to left on all rnds.

Infinity Cowl

●●○○ **EASY**

Finished Measurement:
6½" wide x 56" long
(16.5 cm x 142 cm)

SHOPPING LIST

Yarn (Medium Weight) MEDIUM 4

[7 ounces, 370 yards
(198 grams, 338 meters) per skein]:
☐ 1 skein

Knitting Needles

29" (73.5 cm) Circular,
☐ Size 9 (5.5 mm)

Additional Supplies

☐ Yarn needle

GAUGE INFORMATION

Gauge is not crucial for this project.

TECHNIQUES USED

- YO ***(Photo G, page 7)***
- K2 tog ***(Photo K, page 7)***
- SSK ***(Photos L & M, page 8)***
- S2KP2 ***(Photos N thru P, page 8)***

COWL

First Lace Section

Cast on 22 sts.

Row 1 (Right side)**:** K3, place marker ***(see Markers, page 91)***, ★ YO, K2 tog, K3, SSK, YO, K1; repeat from ★ once **more**, place marker, K3.

Row 2 AND ALL WRONG SIDE ROWS: K3, slip marker, purl to marker, slip marker, K3.

Row 3: K3, slip marker, ★ K1, YO, K2 tog, K1, SSK, YO, K2; repeat from ★ once **more**, slip marker, K3.

Row 5: K3, slip marker, ★ K2, YO, S2KP2, YO, K3; repeat from ★ once **more**, slip marker, K3.

Row 7: K3, slip marker, ★ K2 tog, K1, (YO, K1) twice, SSK, K1; repeat from ★ once **more**, slip marker, K3.

Rows 9-14: Repeat Rows 7 and 8, 3 times.

Row 15: K3, slip marker, ★ YO, K2 tog, K3, SSK, YO, K1; repeat from ★ once **more**, slip marker, K3.

Repeat Rows 2-15 until piece measures approximately 13½" (34.5 cm) from cast on edge, ending by working a **wrong** side row.

Next 4 Rows: Knit across.

FIRST LACE SECTION

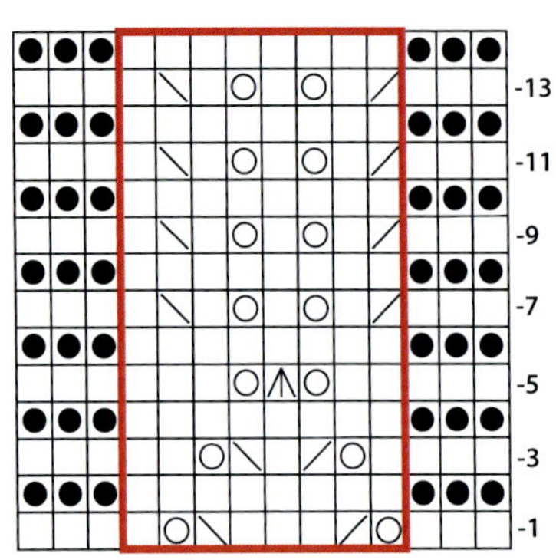

KEY
- knit on RS; purl on WS
- knit on WS
- K2 tog
- SSK
- YO
- S2KP2
- pattern repeat

Repeat Rows 1-14 for pattern.

Follow chart from right to left on RS rows; follow chart from left to right on WS rows.

Second Lace Section

Row 1: K3, slip marker, (YO, K2 tog) to marker, slip marker, K3.

Row 2: K3, slip marker, purl to marker, slip marker, K3.

Row 3: K3, slip marker, (K2 tog, YO) to marker, slip marker, K3.

Row 4: K3, slip marker, purl to marker, slip marker, K3.

Repeat Rows 1-4 for pattern until piece measures approximately 27½" (70 cm) from cast on edge, ending by working a **wrong** side row.

Next 4 Rows: Knit across.

Third Lace Section

Row 1: K3, slip marker, ★ SSK, K1, (YO, K1) twice, K2 tog, K1; repeat from ★ once **more**, slip marker, K3.

Row 2 AND ALL WRONG SIDE ROWS: K3, slip marker, purl to marker, slip marker, K3.

Row 3: K3, slip marker, ★ SSK, YO, K3, YO, K2 tog, K1; repeat from ★ once **more**, slip marker, K3.

Row 5: K3, slip marker, ★ YO, K1, K2 tog, K1, SSK, K1, YO, K1; repeat from ★ once **more**, slip marker, K3.

Row 7: K3, slip marker, ★ K1, YO, K2 tog, K1, SSK, YO, K2; repeat from ★ once **more**, slip marker, K3.

Row 8: K3, slip marker, purl to marker, slip marker, K3.

Repeat Rows 1-8 for pattern until piece measures approximately 41½" (105.5 cm) from cast on edge, ending by working a **wrong** side row.

Next 4 Rows: Knit across.

Fourth Lace Section

Row 1 (Right side)**:** K3, slip marker, ★ K1, YO, SSK, K1; repeat from ★ to marker, slip marker, K3.

Row 2 AND ALL WRONG SIDE ROWS: K3, slip marker, purl to marker, slip marker, K3.

Row 3: K3, slip marker, ★ K2, YO, SSK; repeat from ★ to marker, slip marker, K3.

Row 5: K3, slip marker, ★ SSK, K2, YO; repeat from ★ to marker, slip marker, K3.

Row 7: K3, slip marker, ★ YO, SSK, K2; repeat from ★ to marker, slip marker, K3.

Row 9: K3, slip marker, ★ K2, K2 tog, YO; repeat from ★ to marker, slip marker, K3.

Row 11: K3, slip marker, ★ K1, K2 tog, YO, K1; repeat from ★ to marker, slip marker, K3.

SECOND LACE SECTION

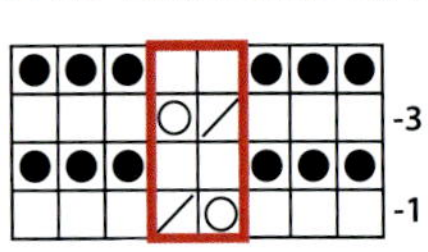

KEY

knit on RS; purl on WS

knit on WS

K2 tog

YO

pattern repeat

Repeat Rows 1-4 for pattern.

Follow chart from right to left on RS rows; follow chart from left to right on WS rows.

THIRD LACE SECTION

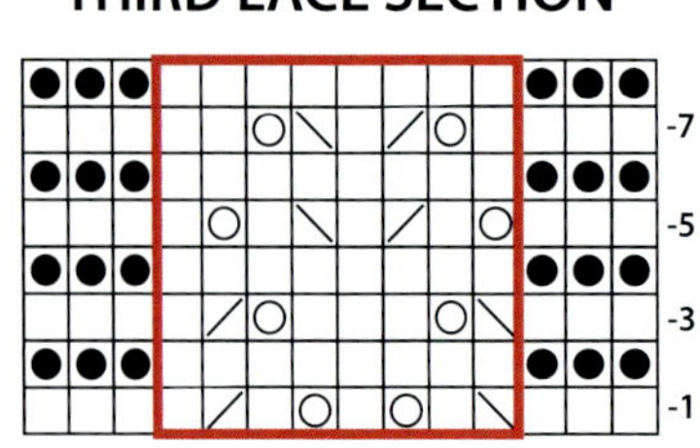

KEY

knit on RS; purl on WS

knit on WS

K2 tog

SSK

YO

pattern repeat

Repeat Rows 1-8 for pattern.

Follow chart from right to left on RS rows; follow chart from left to right on WS rows.

Row 13: K3, slip marker, ★ K2 tog, YO, K2; repeat from ★ to marker, slip marker, K3.

Row 15: K3, slip marker, ★ YO, K2, K2 tog; repeat from ★ to marker, slip marker, K3.

Row 16: K3, slip marker, purl to marker, slip marker, K3.

Repeat Rows 1-16 for pattern until piece measures approximately 55½" (141 cm) from cast on edge, ending by working a **wrong** side row.

Next 4 Rows: Knit across.

Bind off all sts in **knit**.

Finishing

Sew cast on edge to bound off edge.

FOURTH LACE SECTION

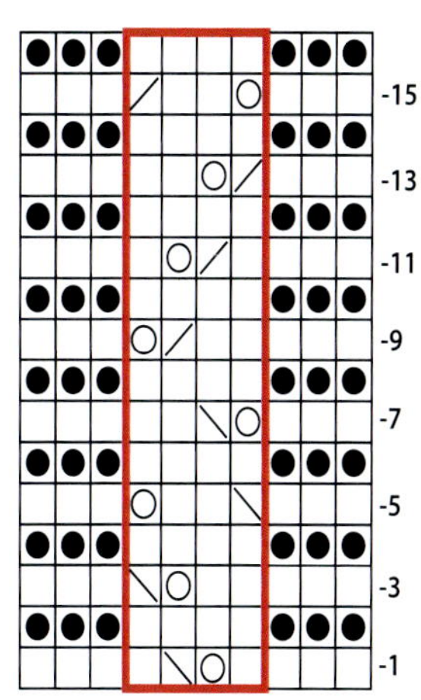

KEY

- knit on RS; purl on WS
- knit on WS
- K2 tog
- SSK
- YO
- pattern repeat

Repeat Rows 1-16 for pattern.

Follow chart from right to left on RS rows; follow chart from left to right on WS rows.

Crop Top

●●○○ EASY

SHOPPING LIST

Yarn (Medium Weight) MEDIUM 4

[3½ ounces, 186 yards

(100 grams, 170 meters) per skein]:

☐ {7-8}{9-10-11} skeins

Knitting Needles

29" (73.5 cm) Circular,

☐ Size 6 (4 mm)

or size needed for gauge

Additional Supplies

☐ Yarn needle

SIZE INFORMATION

Finished Chest Measurement:

{38-44½}{50¾-57¼-63½}"/

{96.5-113}{129-145.5-161.5} cm

Finished Length:

{18-18}{18½-18½-19}"/

{45.5-45.5}{47-47-48.5} cm

Size Note: For ease in following the pattern, we have printed the instructions for each size in a different color:

- Size Small in Blue
- Size Medium in Pink
- Size Large in Green
- Size 1X in Red
- Size 2X in Purple

GAUGE INFORMATION

In pattern,

20 sts and 32 rows = 4" (10 cm)

TECHNIQUES USED

- YO ***(Photo G, page 7)***
- K2 tog ***(Photo K, page 7)***
- SSK ***(Photos L & M, page 8)***
- P2 tog ***(Fig. 10, page 94)***
- SSP ***(Fig. 12, page 94)***

BACK

Lower Band

Cast on {87-102}{116-131-145} sts.

Work in Garter Stitch for 1" (2.5 cm), increasing {10-11}{13-14-16} sts evenly spaced across last row ***(see Increasing Evenly Across A Row, page 92)***: {97-113}{129-145-161} sts.

Body

Row 1 (Right side)**:** P1, ★ P2, SSK, K3, YO, K1, YO, K3, K2 tog, P3; repeat from ★ across.

Row 2 AND ALL WRONG SIDE ROWS: Purl across.

Row 3: P1, ★ P2, SSK, K2, YO, K3, YO, K2, K2 tog, P3; repeat from ★ across.

Row 5: P1, ★ P2, SSK, K1, YO, K5, YO, K1, K2 tog, P3; repeat from ★ across.

Row 7: P1, ★ P2, SSK, YO, K7, YO, K2 tog, P3; repeat from ★ across.

Row 9: K1, ★ YO, K3, K2 tog, P5, SSK, K3, YO, K1; repeat from ★ across.

Row 11: K1, ★ K1, YO, K2, K2 tog, P5, SSK, K2, YO, K2; repeat from ★ across.

Row 13: K1, ★ K2, YO, K1, K2 tog, P5, SSK, K1, YO, K3; repeat from ★ across.

Row 15: K1, ★ K3, YO, K2 tog, P5, SSK, YO, K4; repeat from ★ across.

Row 16: Purl across.

CHART

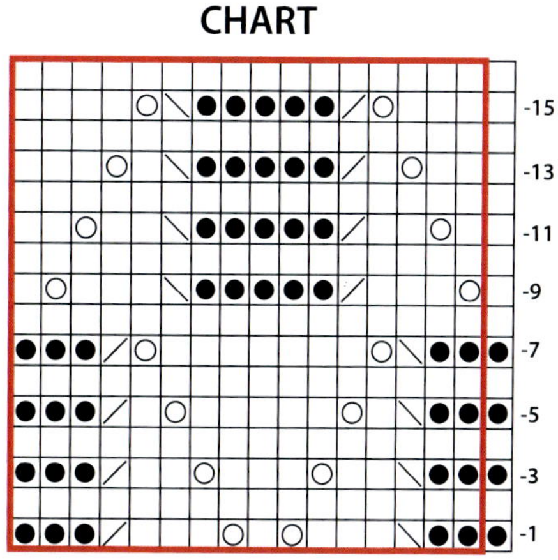

KEY

☐ knit on RS; purl on WS

● purl on RS

╱ K 2tog

╲ SSK

○ YO

▯ pattern repeat

Repeat Rows 1-16 for pattern.

Follow chart from right to left on RS rows; follow chart from left to right on WS rows.

Repeat Rows 1-16 for pattern until piece measures approximately 9" (23 cm) from cast on edge, ending by working a **purl** row.

ARMHOLE SHAPING

Note: Maintain established pattern throughout.

Rows 1 and 2: Bind off {8-8}{16-16-24} sts, work across: {81-97}{97-113-113} sts.

Work even until piece measures approximately {15-15}{15½-15½-16}"/{38-38}{39.5-39.5-40.5} cm from cast on edge, ending by working a **wrong** side row.

NECK SHAPING

Note: Both sides of Neck are worked at the same time, using separate yarn for **each** side.

Row 1: Work across first {25-33}{33-41-41} sts; with second yarn, bind off next 31 sts, work across: {25-33}{33-41-41} sts **each** side.

Rows 2 and 3: Work across to Neck edge; with second yarn, bind off 4 sts, work across: {21-29}{29-37-37} sts **each** side.

Rows 4 and 5: Work across to Neck edge; with second yarn, bind off 2 sts, work across: {19-27}{27-35-35} sts **each** side.

Row 6: Purl across to within 2 sts of Neck edge, SSP; with second yarn, P2 tog, purl across: {18-26}{26-34-34} sts **each** side.

Work even until piece measures approximately {17-17}{17½-17½-18}"/{43-43}{44.5-44.5-45.5} cm from cast on edge, ending by working a **wrong** side row.

SHOULDER SHAPING

Rows 1-6: Bind off {5-6}{6-8-8} sts, work across to Neck edge; with second yarn, work across: {3-8}{8-10-10} sts each side

Row 7: Bind off to Neck edge; with second yarn, work across.

Bind off remaining sts.

FRONT

Work same as Back.

SLEEVE (Make 2)

Lower Band

Cast on 44 sts.

Work in Garter Stitch for 1" (2.5 cm), increasing 5 sts evenly spaced across last row: 49 sts.

Body

Work in pattern same as Back, increasing one st at **each** edge, every {8-8}{6-6-4} rows, {10-15}{9-17-6} times; then increase every {10-10}{8-8-6} rows, {6-1}{9-1-15} time(s): {81-81}{85-85-91} sts.

Work even until Sleeve measures approximately {20½-19¼}{19¼-17¾-18¼}"/{52-49}{49-45-46.5} cm from cast on edge, ending by working a **purl** row.

Bind off all sts in **knit**.

FINISHING

Sew right shoulder seam.

Neckband

With the **right** side facing, pick up 120 sts evenly spaced along neck edge (***Figs. 13a & b, page 94***).

Work in Garter St for ½" (12 mm).

Next Row: Knit across decreasing 12 sts evenly spaced: 108 sts.

Work even until Neckband measures 1" (2.5 cm).

Bind off all sts loosely in **knit**.

Sew left shoulder seam and end of rows on Neckband.

Set in Sleeves.

Weave underarm and side in one continuous seam ***(Fig. 16, page 95)*** leaving Lower Band free on Front and Back for side vents.

Schematic Label	Description	Imperial Measurement / Metric Measurement
A	Chest Measurement	{38-44½}{50¾-57¼-63½}" / {96.5-113}{129-145.5-161.5} cm
B	Body Length to Underarm	9" / 23 cm
C	Body Length to Neck Shaping	{15-15}{15½-15½-16}" / {38-38}{39.5-39.5-40.5} cm
D	Body Length to Shoulder Shaping	{17-17}{17½-17½-18}" / {43-43}{44.5-44.5-45.5} cm
E	Body Width across Shoulders	{15¾-19}{19-22¼-22¼}" / {40-48.5}{48.5-56.5-56.5} cm
F	Neck Width	9" / 23 cm
G	Neck Depth	2" / 5 cm
H	Shoulder Shaping	¾" / 19 mm
I	Sleeve Width at Cuff	9½" / 44 cm
J	Sleeve Length	{20½-19¼}{19¼-17¾-18¼}" / {52-49}{49-45-46.5} cm
K	Sleeve Width at Upper Arm	{15¾-15¾}{16½-16½-17¾}" / {40-40}{42-42-45} cm

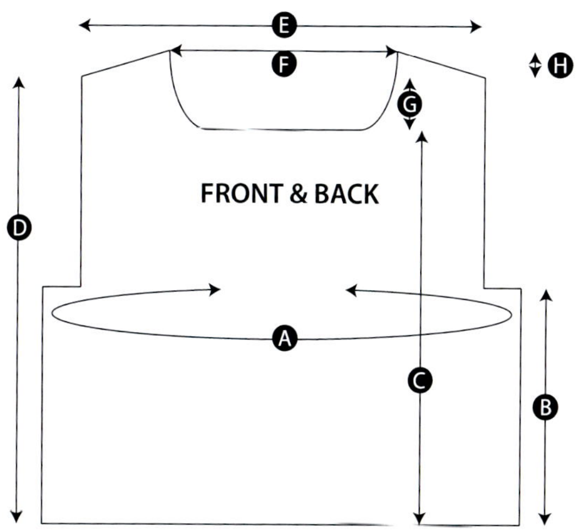

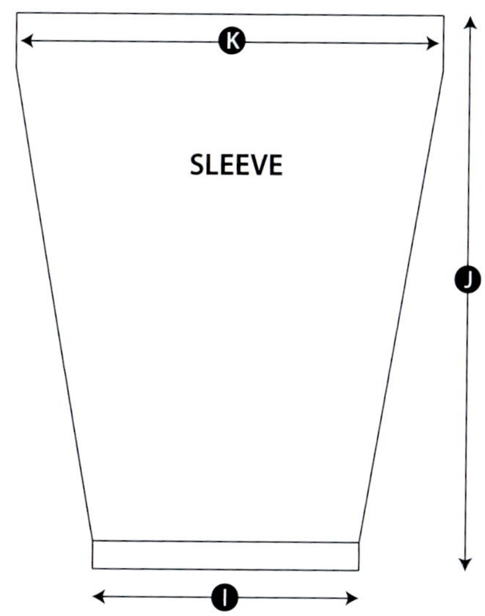

GENERAL INSTRUCTIONS

ABBREVIATIONS

C8B	Cable 8 Back
C8F	Cable 8 Front
CC	Contrasting Color
cm	centimeters
K	knit
M1	make one
MC	Main Color
mm	millimeters
P	purl
PSSO	pass slipped stitch over
P2SSO	pass 2 slipped stitches over
Rnd(s)	Round(s)
RS	right side
S2KP2	slip 2, knit 1, pass 2 slipped stitches over
SSK	slip, slip, knit
SSP	slip, slip, purl
SSSK	slip, slip, slip, knit
st(s)	stitch(es)
tbl	through back loop(s)
tog	together
WS	wrong side
YO	yarn over

SYMBOLS & TERMS

★ — work instructions following ★ as many **more** times as indicated in addition to the first time.

† to † — work all instructions from first † to second † **as many** times as specified.

( ) or **[ ]** — work enclosed instructions **as many** times as specified by the number immediately following **or** work all enclosed instructions in the stitch or space indicated **or** contains explanatory remarks.

colon (:) — the number(s) given after a colon at the end of a row or round denote(s) the number of stitches and spaces you should have on that row or round.

work even — work without increasing or decreasing in the established pattern.

KNIT TERMINOLOGY		
UNITED STATES		INTERNATIONAL
gauge	=	tension
bind off	=	cast off
yarn over (YO)	=	yarn forward (yfwd) **or** yarn around needle (yrn)

Yarn Weight Symbol & Names	LACE 0	SUPER FINE 1	FINE 2	LIGHT 3	MEDIUM 4	BULKY 5	SUPER BULKY 6	JUMBO 7
Type of Yarns in Category	Fingering, size 10 crochet thread	Sock, Fingering, Baby	Sport, Baby	DK, Light Worsted	Worsted, Afghan, Aran	Chunky, Craft, Rug	Super Bulky, Roving	Jumbo, Roving
Knit Gauge Ranges in Stockinette St to 4" (10 cm)	33-40 sts**	27-32 sts	23-26 sts	21-24 sts	16-20 sts	12-15 sts	7-11 sts	6 sts and fewer
Advised Needle Size Range	000 to 1	1 to 3	3 to 5	5 to 7	7 to 9	9 to11	11 to 17	17 and larger

* GUIDELINES ONLY: The chart above reflects the most commonly used gauges and needle sizes for specific yarn categories.

** Lace weight yarns are usually knitted on larger needles to create lacy openwork patterns. Accordingly, a gauge range is difficult to determine. Always follow the gauge stated in your pattern.

GAUGE

Exact gauge is essential for proper size. Before beginning your project, make a sample swatch in the yarn and needle specified in the individual instructions. After completing the swatch, measure it, counting your stitches and rows carefully. If your swatch is larger or smaller than specified, **make another, changing needle size to get the correct gauge.** Keep trying until you find the size needles that will give you the specified gauge.

MARKERS

As a convenience to you, we have used markers to help distinguish the beginning of a pattern. Place markers as instructed. You may use purchased markers or tie a length of contrasting color yarn around the needle. When you reach a marker on each row or round, slip it from the left needle to the right needle; remove it when no longer needed.

HINTS

As in all pieces, good finishing techniques make a big difference in the quality of the piece. Do **not** tie knots. Always start a new ball at the beginning of a row, leaving ends long enough to weave in later.

ZEROS

To consolidate the length of an involved pattern, Zeros are sometimes used so that all sizes can be combined. For example, increase every sixth row 5{1-0} time(s) means the first size would increase 5 times, the second size would increase once, and the largest size would do nothing.

●○○○ **BASIC**	Projects using basic stitches. May include basic increases and decreases.
●●○○ **EASY**	Projects may include simple stitch patterns, color work, and/or shaping.
●●●○ **INTERMEDIATE**	Projects may include involved stitch patterns, color work, and/or shaping.
●●●● **COMPLEX**	Projects may include complex stitch patterns, color work, and/or shaping using a variety of techniques and stitches simultaneously.

KNITTING NEEDLES																			
U.S.	0	1	2	3	4	5	6	7	8	9	10	10½	11	13	15	17	19	35	50
U.K.	13	12	11	10	9	8	7	6	5	4	3	2	1	00	000	---	---	---	---
Metric - mm	2	2.25	2.75	3.25	3.5	3.75	4	4.5	5	5.5	6	6.5	8	9	10	12.75	15	19	25

CIRCULAR KNITTING

Using Circular Needle

When you knit a tube, as for the body of a pullover, you are going to work around on the outside of the circle, with the **right** side of the knitting facing you.

Using a circular needle, cast on all stitches as instructed. Untwist and straighten the stitches on the needle to be sure that the cast on ridge lays on the inside of the needle and never rolls around the needle.

Hold the needle so that the ball of yarn is attached to the stitch closest to the right hand point. Place a marker on the right hand point to mark the beginning of the round.

To begin working in the round, knit the stitches on the left hand point ***(Fig. 1)***.

Continue working each round as instructed without turning the work; but for the first three rounds or so, check to be sure that the cast on edge has not twisted around the needle. If it has, it is impossible to untwist it. The only way to fix this is to rip it out and return to the cast on row.

Fig. 1

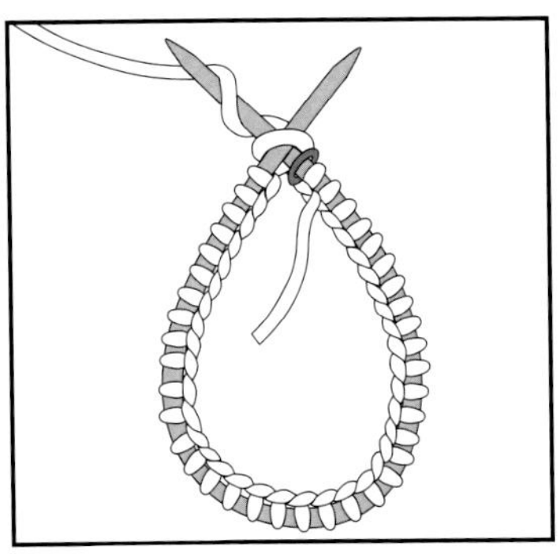

Double Pointed Needles

When working too few stitches to use a circular needle, double pointed needles are required. Divide the stitches between three or four double pointed needles as specified in individual pattern. Being careful not to twist the cast on ridge, form a triangle with the three needles, or a square with the four needles. With the working yarn coming from the stitch on the last needle, work across the stitches on the first needle ***(Fig. 2)***. You will now have an empty needle with which to knit the stitches from the next needle. Work the first stitch of each needle firmly to prevent gaps. Continue working around without turning the work. If there is a yarn over at the end of the needle, take care not to lose it.

Fig. 2

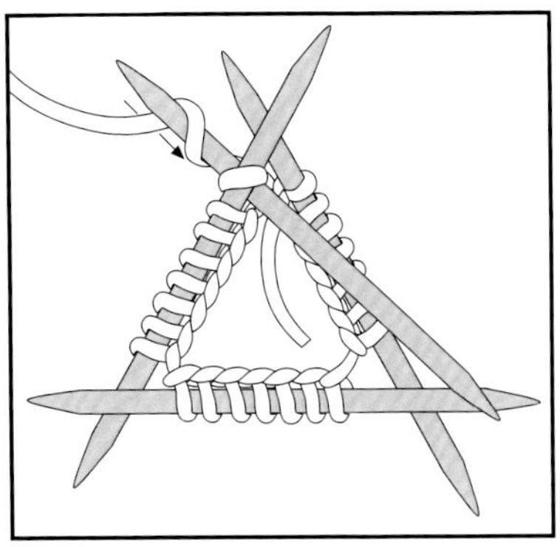

INCREASES

Increasing Evenly Across A Row

Add one to the number of increases required and divide that number into the number of stitches on the needle. Subtract one from the result and the new number is the approximate number of stitches to be worked between each increase. Adjust the number as needed.

Knit Increase

Knit the next stitch but do **not** slip the old stitch off the left needle ***(Fig. 3a)***. Insert the right needle into the **back** loop of the **same** stitch and knit it ***(Fig. 3b)***, then slip the old stitch off the left needle.

Fig. 3a

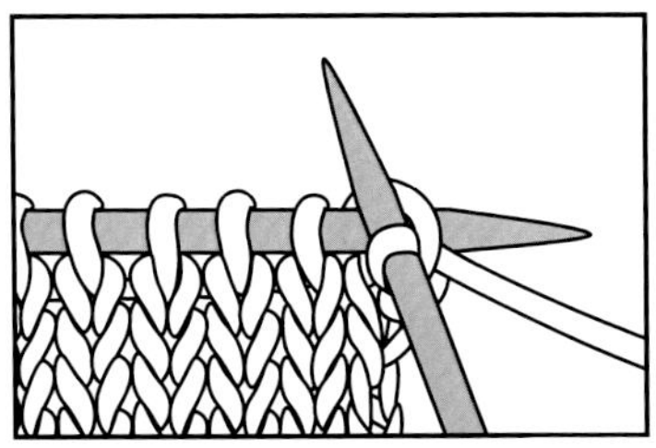

Fig. 3b

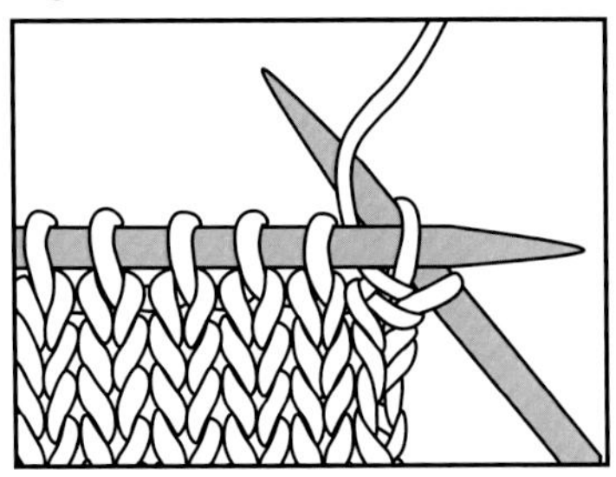

Purl Increase

Purl the next stitch but do **not** slip the old stitch off the left needle. Insert the right needle into the **back** loop of the **same** stitch and purl it *(Fig. 4)*, then slip the old stitch off the left needle.

Fig. 4

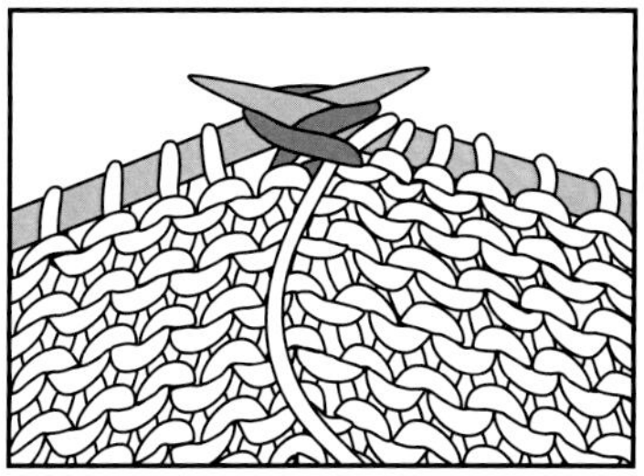

Make One *(abbreviated M1)*

Insert the **left** needle under the horizontal strand between the stitches from the **front** *(Fig. 5a)*. Then **knit** into the **back** of the strand *(Fig. 5b)*.

Fig. 5a

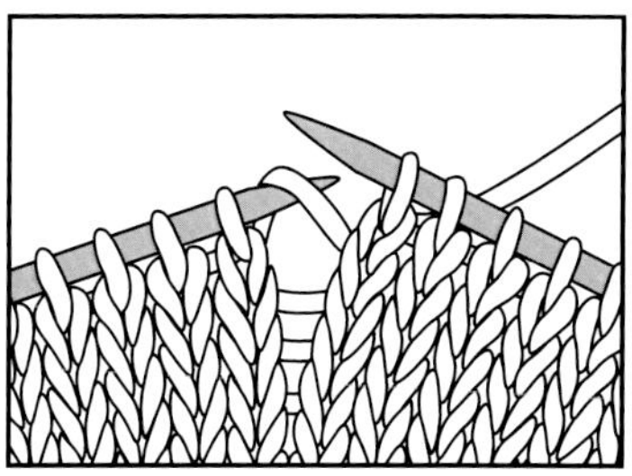

Fig. 5b

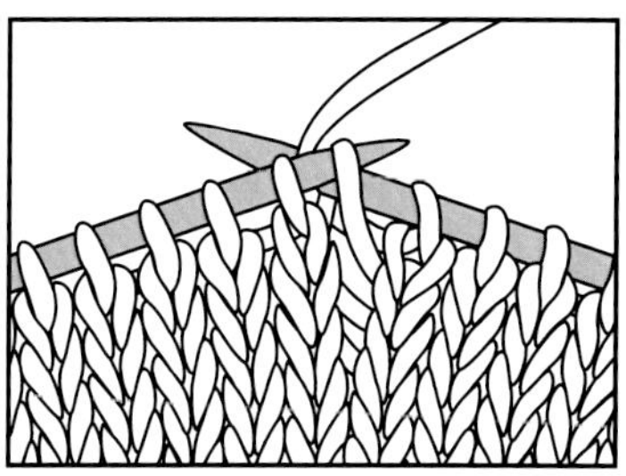

Make One Purl *(abbreviated M1P)*

Insert the **left** needle under the horizontal strand between the stitches from the **back** *(Fig. 6a)*. Then **purl** into the **front** of the strand *(Fig. 6b)*.

Fig. 6a

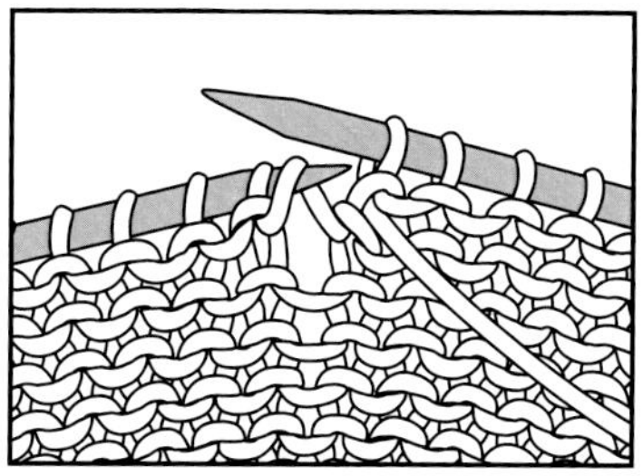

Fig. 6b

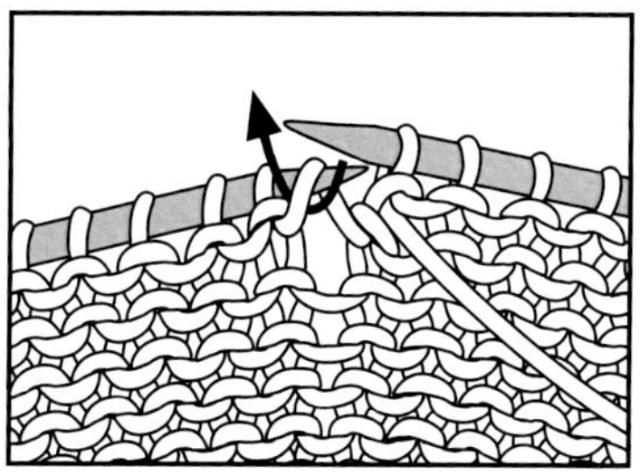

Yarn Over Twice

★ Bring the yarn forward **between** the needles, then back **over** the top of the right hand needle; repeat from ★ once **more**, so that it is now in position to knit the next stitch *(Fig. 7)*.

Fig. 7

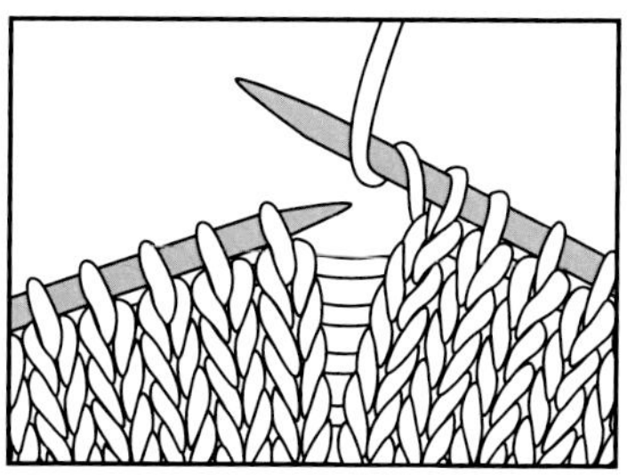

Adding New Stitches

Insert the right needle into the stitch as if to **knit**, yarn over and pull loop through *(Fig. 8a)*, insert the left needle into the loop just worked from **front** to **back** and slip the loop onto the left needle *(Fig. 8b)*. Repeat for the required number of stitches.

Fig. 8a

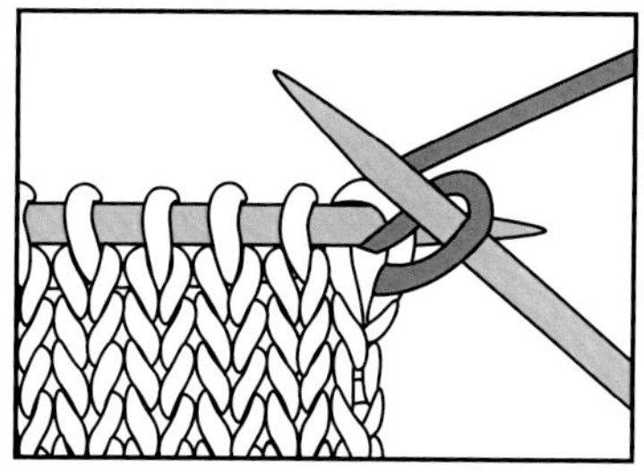

Fig. 8b

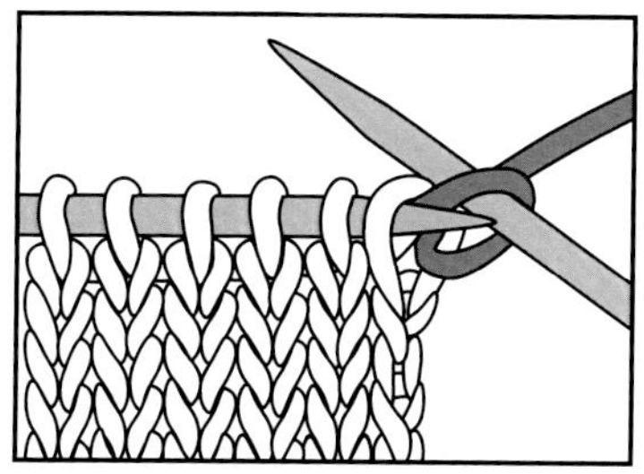

DECREASES

Knit 2 Together Through Back Loop *(abbreviated K2 tog tbl)*

Insert the right needle into the **back** of first two stitches on the left needle from **front** to **back** *(Fig. 9)*, then **knit** them together as if they were one stitch.

Fig. 9

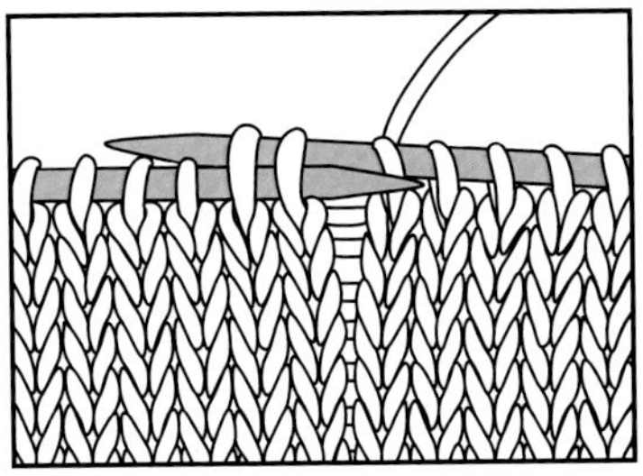

Purl 2 Together *(abbreviated P2 tog)*

Insert the right needle into the **front** of the first two stitches on the left needle as if to **purl** *(Fig. 10)*, then **purl** them together as if they were one stitch.

Fig. 10

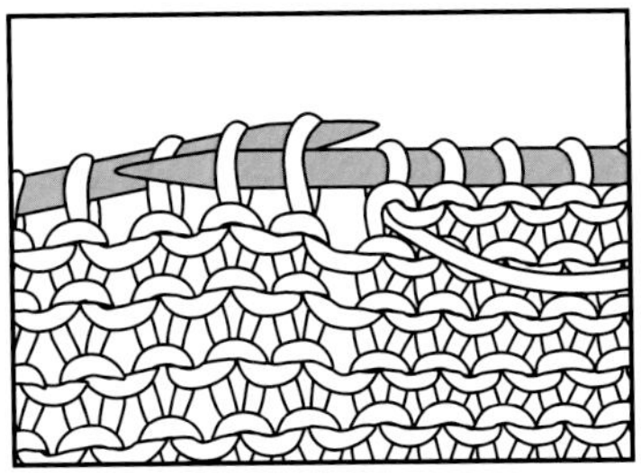

Knit 3 Together *(abbreviated K3 tog)*

Insert the right needle into the **front** of the first three stitches on the left needle as if to **knit** *(Fig. 11)*, then **knit** them together as if they were one stitch.

Fig. 11

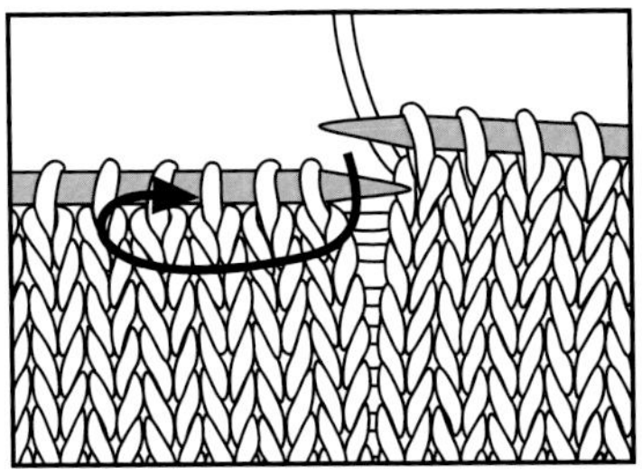

Slip, Slip, Purl *(abbreviated SSP)*

Separately slip two stitches as if to **knit**. Place these two stitches back onto the left needle. Insert the right needle into the **back** of both stitches from **back** to **front** *(Fig. 12)* and **purl** them together as if they were one stitch.

Fig. 12

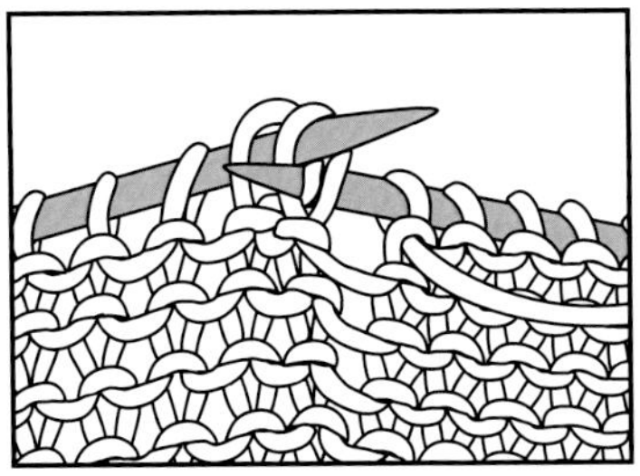

PICKING UP STITCHES

When instructed to pick up stitches, insert the needle from the **front** to the **back** under two strands at the edge of the worked piece *(Figs. 13a & b)*. Put the yarn around the needle as if to **knit**, then bring the needle with the yarn back through the stitch to the right side, resulting in a stitch on the needle.

Repeat this along the edge, picking up the required number of stitches.

A crochet hook may be helpful to pull yarn through.

Fig. 13a

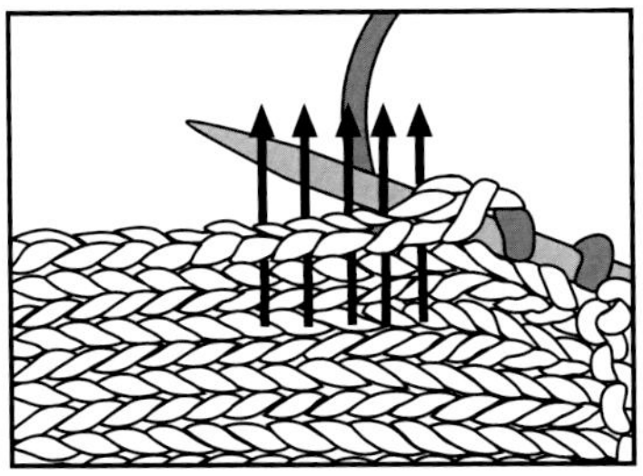

Fig. 13b

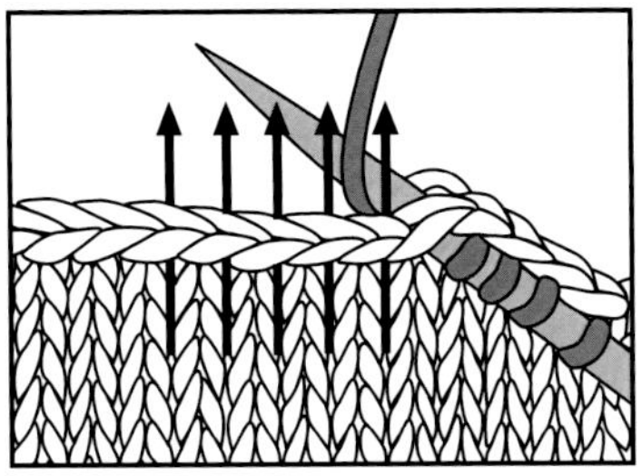

WORKING INTO THE CHAIN

Insert the needle into the back ridge of each chain *(Fig. 14)*.

Fig. 14

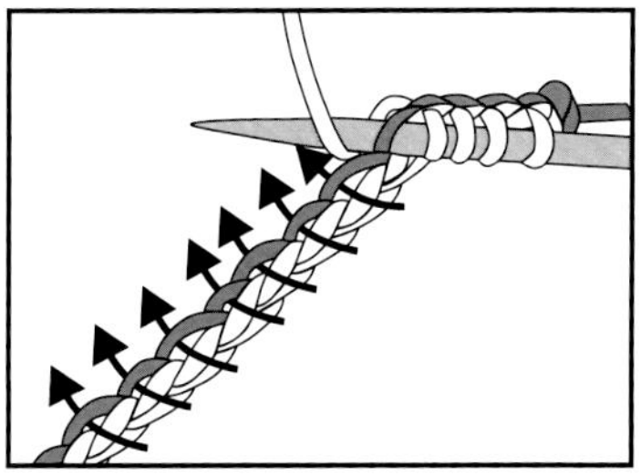

3-NEEDLE BIND OFF

Holding pieces with **right** sides together and needles parallel to each other, insert a third needle as if to **knit** into the first stitch on the front needle **and** into the first stitch on the back needle *(Fig. 15)*. Knit these two stitches together and slip them off the needle. ★ Knit the next stitch on each needle together and slip them off the needle. To bind off, insert the left needle into the first stitch on the right needle and pull the first stitch over the second stitch and off the right needle; repeat from ★ across until all of the stitches on the front needle have been bound off.

Fig. 15

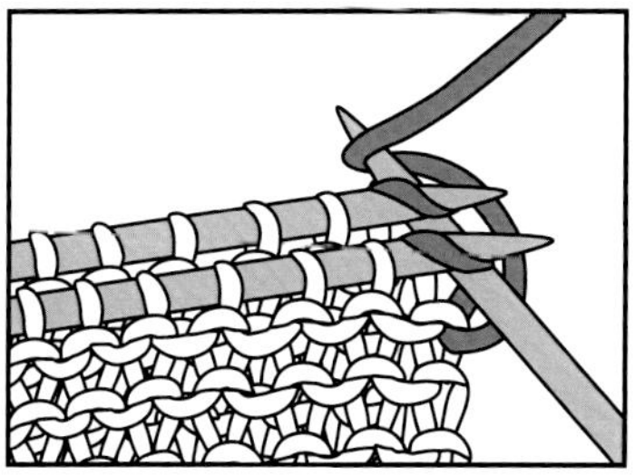

WEAVING SEAMS

With the **right** side of both pieces facing you and edges even, sew through both sides once to secure the seam. Insert the needle under the bar between the first and second stitches on the row and pull the yarn through *(Fig. 16)*. Insert the needle under the next bar on the second side. Repeat from side to side, being careful to match rows. If the edges are different lengths, it may be necessary to insert the needle under two bars at one edge.

Fig. 16

FRINGE

Cut a piece of cardboard 12" (30.5 cm) wide and ½" (12 mm) longer than you want your finished fringe to be. Wind the yarn **loosely** and **evenly** lengthwise around the cardboard until the card is filled, then cut across one end; repeat as needed.

Hold together as many strands as specified in individual instructions; fold in half.

With **wrong** side facing and using a crochet hook, draw the folded end up through a stitch and pull the loose ends through the folded end *(Fig. 17a)*; draw the knot up **tightly** *(Fig. 17b)*. Repeat, spacing as specified in individual instructions.

Lay flat on a hard surface and trim the ends.

Fig. 17a

Fig. 17b

YARN INFORMATION

The items in this book were made using a variety of yarns. Any brand of the specific weight of yarn may be used. It is best to refer to the yardage/meters when determining how many balls or skeins to purchase. Remember, to achieve the same look, it is the weight of yarn that is important, not the brand of yarn.

For your convenience, listed below are the specific yarns used to create our photography models.Because yarn manufacturers make frequent changes to their product lines, you may sometimes find it necessary to use a substitute yarn or to search for the discontinued product at alternate suppliers (locally or online).

STRIPED COWL
Red Heart® Amore™
Cream - #6316 Chamomile
Terra Cotta - #6259 Chai
Gray - #6340 Whisper

SLOUCHY HAT
Lion Brand® Color Made Easy®
#184 Millennial

CAP SLEEVE TOP
Red Heart® Amore™
#6638 Restful

SCARF
Red Heart® Hygge™
#8631 Aloe

BABY CARDI
Red Heart® With Love®
#1711 Cameo

SKINNY SCARF
Lion Brand® Coboo
#102 Pale Pink

BIAS WRAP
Lion Brand® Feels Like Butta
Pale Aqua - #106 Ice
Medium Blue - #108 Dusty Blue
Teal - #178 Teal

TWO-COLOR SHAWL
Lion Brand® Beautiful You
#150 Pumice Stone
#184 Spanish Villa

LACE BORDER TOP
Lion Brand® Coboo
#149 Silver

LONG VEST
Red Heart® Comfort®
#7002 Grey/Silver

ASSYMETRICAL SHAWL
Lion Brand® Wrap Star
#204 Lisa

SAMPLER CARDI
Red Heart® Amore™
#6316 Chamomile

HOODIE
Red Heart® Hygge™
#8319 Rust

MANDALA SHAWL
Lion Brand® Mandala
#210 Pegasus

BOHO VEST
Red Heart® Comfort®
#3228 Papaya

BABY BLANKET
Red Heart® With Love®
#1936 Terracotta

INFINITY COWL
Red Heart® With Love®
#1303 Aran

CROP TOP
Lion Brand® 24/7 Cotton®
#149 Silver

The Cataloging-in-Publication Data is on file with the Library of Congress.

We have made every effort to ensure that these instructions are accurate and complete. We cannot, however, be responsible for human error, typographical mistakes, or variations in individual work.

Production Team: Project Manager - Linda A. Daley; Instructional/ Technical Editor - Joan Beebe; Graphic Artist - Angela Ormsby Stark; Photo Stylist - Lori Wenger; and Photographer - Jason Masters.

Made in U.S.A.